N E W
FOOD FOR
THOUGHT

Jane Stimpson

NEW
FOOD FOR
THOUGHT

With illustrations by

Yvonne Chambers and Maxwell Dasey

ANDRE DEUTSCH

First published in Great Britain in 1994 by
André Deutsch Limited
106 Great Russell Street
London WC1B 3LJ

Second impression September 1995

Design by Jeffrey Sains
Typeset by Falcon Graphic Art Ltd

ISBN 0 233 98860 2

Cataloguing-in-Publication data available for this title from the British Library

Printed in Great Britain by
St Edmundsbury Press, Bury St Edmunds, Suffolk

To Alex

for his love and support

ACKNOWLEDGEMENTS

I would sincerely like to express my thanks to all those who have helped with the creation of this book:

Vanessa Garrett and Jurek, the owners of Food For Thought, who have always enthusiastically given me a free hand to experiment and develop recipes at the restaurant.

Charlie Damant, without whom the book would not have got off the ground. For the laborious hours of typing the recipes and deciphering my appalling handwriting, for his contribution in writing the Foreword and as acting as a sounding board for ideas and inspirations and helping to achieve some of them.

My colleagues at Food For Thought for making it such a fun place to work and my thanks particularly to Steve and Jill for contributing some recipes to the book.

My parents and brother for their constant support and belief in me.

All my friends who have been dragged round for countless dinner parties and tastings, particularly my buddy Colette Scully for her practical help and 'words of wisdom'. Also Jennifer Gaffney for always allowing me a monopoly on the fridge.

I am indebted to Maxwell and Yvonne who, I feel, have created a stunning jacket design and illustrations.

Lastly a huge thank you to André Deutsch for publishing the book and to Zoë Ross, my editor, for her tireless work and support and for sharing my vision of a *New Food For Thought*.

I would like to thank Holland and Barrett for their enthusiasm in helping to publicise the book and I recommend them as a source for many of the ingredients that are useful for the budding vegetarian cook.

Achilles Achillios worked for many years at Food For Thought, doing everything from washing-up to chopping vegetables and managing the restaurant until he left to set up his own company, Chalice Foods. Several of his products are used in these recipes.

CONTENTS

FOREWORD

by Charlie Damant

Alan, who has been coming to Food For Thought every lunchtime for eight years, handed over his Christmas card. I opened it up and read: 'To all the friendly and helpful staff at Food For Thought'. Underneath was a completely blank space. I looked up and his face broke into a wide grin. 'Well, what did you expect? You haven't got my favourite flapjacks in today!'

Food For Thought engenders fierce loyalty, pride and reverence, along with a healthy sense of humour. Although the restaurant is small and often rather cramped, we regard ourselves as the best vegetarian restaurant in London, as do our regular customers, demonstrated by their willingness to accept the restaurant's many eccentricities to experience delicious food.

When I first arrived at Food For Thought, just out of university, I didn't know what to expect. On my first day I was so nervous I could hardly speak but within minutes of arriving I knew that I was going to enjoy myself. Jane, the author of this cookbook, played a series of terrible, unrepeatable practical jokes on me and I was soon part of the family of people who love the restaurant, for what it does and how it does it.

Food For Thought was started in 1974 by Margot Boyce-White. At that time, Covent Garden was an area which seemed to be in a state of terminal decline. Margot bravely invested in an old banana ripening warehouse and turned it into, in vegetarian terms, a mini legend. Alongside the Neal's Yard complex it was to become the vital heart that has helped pump life and success into Covent Garden.

In 1976, my father and stepmother, John and Jane Damant, met Margot in France. They were, at the time, trying to eke out a living across the Channel while Margot was on a much needed holiday. She had become tired of the ongoing problems running a restaurant inevitably presents and offered to sell up. John and Jane leapt at the chance and in January 1977 found themselves opening for their first day's business. Initially they thought the restaurant should revert back to serving meat and fish but in the second week a dancer from one of the many nearby theatres said to John: 'You aren't going to change anything about the food, are you? This place is a Godsend.' My father, desperate not to lose customers, quickly replied 'No! Nothing at all!' and thus Food For Thought's fate was sealed. In 1981, after an incredibly successful four years, they handed the running of the restaurant over to my stepsister Vanessa and her Polish husband, Jurek. A year later they were joined by Vanessa's brother, Guy and together formed the partnership that was going to further establish the restaurant's unique reputation.

Whilst Guy, with his impeccable talent for wit and mimicry, charmed the customers and staff alike, Vanessa dealt adeptly with the complexities of running a profitable business in the difficult and competitive environment that Covent Garden had now become. Jurek, meanwhile, would be working all hours, buying the vegetables fresh from New Covent Garden Market, delivering them to the restaurant at seven o'clock in the morning, repairing equipment and rushing all manner of ingredients to the chefs.

In 1987 Guy, along with Food For Thought chef Kit Norman, compiled the first Food For Thought cookbook. The remarkable success of the book underlines how important a contribution the restaurant has made in the field of vegetarian cooking. Guy left Food For Thought in 1989 to start a very successful delicatessen in Crediton, Devon. Vanessa and Jurek continued running the restaurant and in 1993 bought it from John and Jane.

In the last two decades, Covent Garden has grown and developed beyond recognition to become the smartest and most diverse shopping area in London. Neal Street, where the restaurant is situated, is now described as the Carnaby Street of the nineties, with such illustrious designers as John Richmond and Michiko Koshino setting up next to The Kite Store, The Astrology Shop and The Bead Shop and many other weird and wonderful places. And there, in the middle, is Food For Thought, with its semi-permanent queue and manic staff, trying as hard as possible to retain a semblance of dignity amidst the throng. Whilst customers wait, clutching their bowls of hotpot and plates of mixed salad, straining to see where and when the next seat is going to become available, some member of staff is constantly squeezing between them, trying to keep the water jugs full, the tables clear and pass along a steady supply of dishes to be washed up. In the cramped kitchen upstairs, the chefs emerge from among great steaming cauldrons, frantically making up a stir-fry in response to an urgent shout from one of the servers, whilst making up stocks for the afternoon main course and planning the next day's menu. Even after eighteen months of working here I still cannot quite believe the quantities of each dish that they make and that people come from all over the world to try it.

We are now in our twentieth year and have served approximately six million dishes to four million customers. The format has not really changed from those first days in 1974, with the restaurant opening at midday and continuing until 8.00pm with no break. We also serve breakfast now and open on Saturday and Sunday, although on Sundays we close at 4.00pm.

We continue to outsmart our rivals and prosper in the face of increasingly fierce competition, as we rely on the consummate skill of exceptional chefs. It has been a privilege to work with a chef of the competence, quality and imagination of Jane and it has been a further privilege to help her with this cookbook. To me, the book illustrates the diversity and the delight not only of Food For Thought but of vegetarian cooking as a whole, and proves that vegetarian food is neither boring nor tasteless but instead magnificent, exotic and adventurous. I am certain you will gain much pleasure from using this cookbook but if you want to experience the food without the effort of cooking it, come and see us!

INTRODUCTION

It must have been in 1989 when I received a particularly irate telephone call from Linda McCartney. I had just taken part in a tasting for a national newspaper that involved commenting on a dozen vegetarian convenience products from various supermarkets. I had awarded the two McCartney products the lowest possible mark. The basis for my complaints were the use of TVP (textured vegetable protein) to create a vegetarian dish that looked and tasted like meat (a very sixties concept), the minimal use of vegetables and the fact that the dishes were not nutritionally balanced, providing merely protein (something that is not required in excess, as was thought some years ago). Unfortunately for both of us, ruthless editing had omitted all of these explanations, stating merely '0 out of 10 – disgusting!', thus precipitating Linda's call.

This story (with no disrespect to Mrs McCartney) demonstrates how vegetarian food has changed and people's expectations along with it. Gone are the meat substitutes and the heavy use of pulses, which presented dishes with an overriding brown colour. New vegetarian food has taken on a very international flavour and utilises the vast range of exotic fruits and vegetables now available, generating food that is both well-balanced and attractively presented.

Many of these changes have occurred in the seven years that have elapsed since the first Food For Thought cookbook was published, making a new book imperative. That, coupled with the regular pleas from customers of 'When is the new cookbook coming out?', spurred me on.

New Food For Thought consists of a few core recipes that have been an integral part of the restaurant in some shape or form for the past twenty years, but principally it presents new trends and vogues in cookery with particular emphasis on the influences from the Mediterranean, for example the roasting of vegetables and ingredients such as balsamic vinegar, rocket, lambs lettuce and sundried tomatoes. Due to the very large quantities of each dish that are produced at Food For Thought these ingredients are used sparingly to enable the prices to be kept low. I have included many recipes that I have built up over the years that lend themselves to smaller numbers and are more suitable for dinner parties and buffets.

There are a few points to remember when using the book:

- All the vegetables used (unless otherwise stated) are fresh. Creating a dish of the finest flavour and quality can only be achieved by using fresh produce.

- The Ⓥ symbol attached to some recipes indicates a vegan dish, containing no dairy products or animal derived products (all recipes including honey are termed as non-vegan). The ⓦⓕ symbol denotes a wheatfree dish with no products deriving from wheat and suitable, therefore, for the increasing number of people with an allergy to wheat.

- Measurements are with dessertspoons and teaspoons rather than tablespoons. Cooking temperatures, weights and measures have been roughly rounded up or down during conversion.

- The weights for vegetables are all based on raw produce and none of the vegetables are peeled unless specifically stated (this includes root ginger). The nutrients of vegetables lie just under the skin so by peeling them the nutritional value is reduced.

- Tomato purée used is always double concentrate.

Lastly, like any cookbook, the recipes should only be treated as a guideline. They represent *my* tastes and suggestions which may not always coincide with yours. But I hope I have encouraged you to be confident and experimental with every one of the following ideas.

SOUPS

SOUPS

Of all the food that Food For Thought produces, it is probably the soups that consistently prove to be the most popular. Cooked in enormous pots, two different soups are produced each day reflecting every season.

Soups come in a multitude of guises: light and nutritious with delicately prepared vegetables tantalising the taste buds just in time for the next course; thick, wholesome, earthy pots of steaming broth, blended and finished with fresh herbs, dairy products, alcohol, nuts or seeds; then, of course, the 'meal in itself' soup packed with goodness and laden with vegetables, pulses or grains that float in a richly flavoured stock. Finally, there is the cold soup, fantastic for warm summer evenings or picnics in the sun, served ice-cold with croutons and a swirl of cream, yoghurt or fresh herbs to garnish.

The key to creating good soups lies in the quality of the stock. As a rule use a mixture of vegetables, for example carrots, parsnips, peppers, leeks or celery, with a bayleaf and peppercorns. Bring to the boil and gently simmer for approximately forty-five minutes before straining. This will ensure a tasty stock suitable for any soup recipe. If time is precious and stock cubes are preferred, be selective as the quality varies tremendously according to the brand. Check the side of the packet for the listing of ingredients, ensuring no E numbers and a minimal amount of salt. Many stock cubes have a very high percentage of salt which completely changes the balance of seasoning within the dish.

Soups are a true delight to produce and may be excelled at whether a complete novice or a superchef, drawing gasps of delight and surprise when served.

BEETROOT, COCONUT AND LIME SOUP (v)(wf)

(Serves 4)

½ oz (12g) soya margarine	13 oz (375g) cooked beetroot, roughly chopped (without vinegar)
1 onion, finely chopped	
1 stick celery, thinly sliced	juice of 2 limes
3 oz (75g) creamed coconut	salt and pepper
1¼ pint (150ml) vegetable stock	small quantity of fresh coriander
	chives to garnish

1. In a saucepan melt the margarine then add the onion and celery. Cook until soft.

2. Add the creamed coconut, stock, beetroot and lime juice. Bring up to the boil stirring occasionally, ensuring that the coconut does not stick to the base of the saucepan.

3. Using an electric blender, process until completely smooth. Return to the saucepan and stir in the salt, pepper and finely chopped coriander.

4. Bring up to temperature then garnish with chopped chives.

Cook's tips:
This soup sounds like a weird combination but it works beautifully. It is equally good hot or cold and because of the colour makes a stunning first course.

BREADFRUIT AND YOGHURT SOUP ⓦⓕ

(Serves 4)

1 oz (25g) butter	1 lb (450g) breadfruit, peeled, cored and finely chopped
1 red onion, finely chopped	
1 onion, finely chopped	2 pints (1.2 litres) vegetable stock
1 clove garlic, crushed	10 oz (275g) natural yoghurt
½ large green chilli, finely chopped	few leaves of fresh coriander to garnish
1 large carrot, grated	salt and pepper

1. In a large saucepan melt the butter and fry the onions, garlic, chilli and carrot. Cook until the onions are soft.

2. Stir in the breadfruit and stock. Cook for approximately 15 minutes until the breadfruit is tender. Cool, then using an electric blender, process the soup, adding the yoghurt during blending.

3. Season with salt and pepper. Garnish with coriander.

Cook's tips:
This soup was inspired after a trip to the Grenadines where breadfruit trees grow in abundance. The soup has a thick, fairly starchy consistency and is delicious served cold although it can also be eaten hot. Beware – heat very gently so the soup does not curdle.

Breadfruit can be bought from street markets, Caribbean stores and large supermarkets.

CARIBBEAN CALALLOO SOUP (v) (wf)

(Serves 4)

splash of oil	½ block of coconut cream
1 onion, finely chopped	1 dessertspoon tomato purée
2 cloves garlic, finely chopped	2 pints (1.2 litres) vegetable stock
1 teaspoon turmeric	1 oz (25g) fresh coriander
4 oz (100g) carrot or pumpkin, diced	8 oz (225g) calalloo or fresh spinach, finely shredded
4 oz (100g) sweet potato or yam, diced	salt and pepper

1. Put the oil in a saucepan with the onion, garlic and turmeric. Sauté until soft.

2. Add the remaining ingredients (except the spinach and coriander), cover and simmer for about 15 minutes until the vegetables are tender.

3. Add spinach and finely chopped coriander then cook for a further 2 minutes until the leaves are bright green.

4. Season and serve.

Cook's tips:
Calalloo leaves are the young leaves of the dasheen family. It is similar in appearance and taste to spinach but the leaf is much bigger, with a large stalk that runs through the leaf. If not available (and only markets usually stock it), then spinach is an ideal alternative. Calalloo should never be eaten raw as it makes you very unwell!

CARROT AND LENTIL SOUP

(Serves 4)

1 oz (25g) soya margarine	4 oz (100g) red lentils
1 onion, finely chopped	1 teaspoon yeast extract
1 stick of celery, thinly sliced	1 dessertspoon tomato purée
a few sprigs of thyme, pulled off the stalk and chopped	1 dessertspoon soy sauce
1 large carrot, grated	4 oz (100g) vegetarian cheddar cheese, grated
2 pints (1.2 litres) vegetable stock	salt and pepper

1. In a large saucepan melt the margarine and fry the onion, celery and thyme until soft. Stir in the carrot and cook for a few more minutes.

2. Add the stock, lentils, yeast extract, tomato purée and soy sauce. Cook for approximately 15 minutes until the lentils are light and fluffy.

3. Season and stir in the grated cheese just before serving.

CARROT AND TAHINI SOUP ⓥ

(Serves 4)

1 oz (25g) soya margarine	1 lb (450g) carrots, grated
1 onion, finely chopped	1 dessertspoon tomato purée
1 stick of celery, thinly sliced	3 dessertspoons light tahini
1 teaspoon ground cumin	1 dessertspoon soy sauce
1 dessertspoon white flour	½ oz (12g) fresh coriander
2 pints (1.2 litres) vegetable stock	salt and pepper

1. In a large saucepan melt the margarine and add the onion, celery and cumin. Cook until soft. Reduce the heat and stir in the flour. Cook gently for a few minutes.

2. Add the stock plus the carrots and tomato purée. Cook until the carrots are soft.

3. Using an electric blender, process the soup, adding the tahini slowly until completely smooth.

4. Return to the saucepan. Season with soy sauce, fresh coriander, salt and pepper. Heat gently and serve.

Cook's tips:
Tahini is a paste of blended sesame seeds, of a similar consistency to peanut butter. It can be bought from health food stores or large supermarkets and comes in two varieties, light and dark.

Tahini can curdle a sauce or soup but if flour has been used they can be rescued by blending.

CAULIFLOWER, COCONUT AND LIME SOUP ⓥ ⓦ

(Serves 4)

splash of oil	1½ pints (900 ml) vegetable stock
1 onion, finely chopped	4 oz (100g) coconut cream
1 leek, finely sliced	1 small cauliflower, cored and finely sliced
4 oz (100g) sweet potato, grated	
½ fresh green chilli, crushed	juice of ½ lime
1 teaspoon turmeric	1 oz (25g) fresh coriander
1 clove garlic, crushed	salt and pepper

1. In a saucepan place the oil, onion, leek, sweet potato, chilli, turmeric and garlic. Cook the mixture until it is soft, reducing the heat and adding a little stock if the mixture begins to stick to the pan.

2. Add the stock, coconut cream, cauliflower and lime juice. Bring up to the boil and cook for approximately 10 minutes.

3. Using an electric blender, process the soup, leaving the texture fairly coarse.

4. Finish with finely chopped coriander and season to taste.

Cook's tips:
Coconut and lime is a superb combination and complements many different vegetables. Always avoid cooking cauliflower for too long as the smell changes and becomes distinctly less attractive!

CHINESE THREE MUSHROOM SOUP (wf)

(Serves 4)

splash of sesame oil	1 dessertspoon tomato purée
1 onion, cut in quarters and thinly sliced	1 teaspoon honey
	1 dessertspoon tamari
2 cloves garlic, crushed	3 oz (75g) shitake mushrooms, thinly sliced
1 dessertspoon sesame seeds, ground in a coffee grinder or pestle and mortar	3 oz (75g) oyster mushrooms, thickly sliced
1 oz (25g) root ginger, finely chopped	2 oz (50g) button mushrooms, thinly sliced
½ pint (300ml) dry sherry	8 spring onions, cut into thick diagonal slices
1 pint (600ml) vegetable stock	

1. Place the oil, onion, garlic, sesame seeds and root ginger in a saucepan. Cook on a medium heat until soft.

2. Add the sherry, stock, tomato purée, honey and tamari and continue cooking until the purée has dissolved throughout the soup.

3. Stir in the mushrooms and spring onions and continue cooking until the mushrooms are just tender.

4. Season to taste and serve.

Cook's tips:
The appearance of the **oyster mushroom** is very beautiful. It is named after the oyster because of its shape and its greyish blue colour (you can also buy yellow and pink ones in the supermarket). They are very tender but do not really have an outstanding flavour, however they contribute to the look of the finished dish.

Shitake mushrooms have a firm texture, a fairly strong taste and are quite 'meaty' when cooked. They can be bought dried and are just as good to use as such in this recipe, but make sure they are fully rehydrated (soft and tender) by the time the soup is to be served.

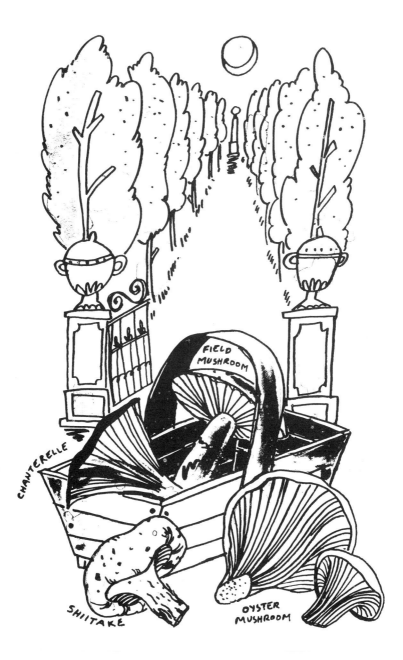

CORN CHOWDER WITH POTATO AND PEPPERS

(Serves 4)

1 oz (25g) butter	11 oz (300g) can of sweetcorn, drained
1 onion, finely chopped	
1 clove garlic, crushed	1 leek, finely chopped
a few sprigs fresh thyme, pulled off the stalk	1 small potato, peeled and cut into cubes
¼ teaspoon ground nutmeg	½ green pepper, cored, de-seeded and cut into very thin strips
1 heaped dessertspoon white flour	
1 pint (600ml) vegetable stock	5 fl oz (140ml) single cream

1. Place the butter, onion, garlic, fresh thyme and nutmeg in a large saucepan. Cook gently until the butter has melted and the mixture is soft.

2. Reduce the heat and stir in the flour. Cook on a low heat until the texture of the roux has changed and it resembles breadcrumbs.

3. Slowly stir in the vegetable stock and half the sweetcorn. Using an electric blender, process until smooth.

4. Add the potato, pepper and leek and cook until the potato is soft. Add the remaining sweetcorn and single cream. Season to taste, heat gently and serve.

CREAM OF MUSHROOM

(Serves 4)

1 oz (25g) butter	8 oz (225g) mushrooms, finely sliced
1 onion, finely chopped	½ pint (300ml) milk
2 sticks of celery, finely chopped	2 dessertspoons soy sauce
2 teaspoons paprika	1 heaped dessertspoon tomato purée
2 cloves garlic, crushed	10 fl oz (280ml) single cream
2 stalks of fresh rosemary, pulled off the stalk and chopped	
1 heaped dessertspoon white flour	

1. Melt the butter in a saucepan and fry the onion, celery, paprika, garlic and fresh rosemary. Cook for approximately 10 minutes until the ingredients are soft. Reduce the heat and stir in the flour.

2. Cook for a couple of minutes before adding the mushrooms (reserve 3 oz/75g), milk, soy sauce and tomato purée. Heat gently until the mushrooms are tender and the soup has begun to thicken.

3. Using an electric blender, process the soup whilst adding the cream. Season and sprinkle in remaining chopped mushrooms. Bring up to temperature and serve.

Cook's tips:
Finely chopped basil is wonderful to serve on top of each bowl as a garnish.

FRENCH PEASANT SOUP

(Serves 4)

splash of olive oil	1 leek, finely chopped
1 onion, finely chopped	½ potato, cubed
1 clove garlic, crushed	1 carrot, cubed
1 lb (450g) tomatoes, cut into quarters	2 oz (50g) haricot beans (soaked overnight then simmered for 1 hour until soft. Drain and rinse well)
2 dessertspoons tomato purée	
1 pint (600ml) vegetable stock	
1 teaspoon Dijon mustard	splash of soy sauce
1 dessertspoon Chalice pesto	1 oz (25g) Parmesan cheese
3 oz (75g) French beans, topped, tailed and cut in half	½ oz (12g) fresh basil
	salt and pepper

1. Place the oil in a saucepan with the onion, garlic and tomatoes. Cook for 5–10 minutes until completely soft and resembling a pulp.

2. Stir in the Dijon mustard, tomato purée, pesto and stock. Using an electric blender, process the soup until smooth.

3. Add the leek, carrot, potato and French beans and continue to cook for 10 minutes until the vegetables are tender.

4. Stir in the cooked haricot beans and season with a splash of soy sauce, Parmesan cheese, fresh basil and salt and pepper. Bring gently up to temperature and serve.

Cook's tips:
This is a very hearty soup and served with some crusty French bread makes an excellent meal. Tinned haricot beans are a quick and good alternative to the dried variety.

GAZPACHO (v) (wf)

(Serves 4)

2 tablespoons olive oil	**GARNISH:**
1 lb (450g) ripe plum tomatoes, cut into quarters	¼ cucumber, diced
2 cloves garlic	½ red onion, diced
½ red onion, roughly chopped	½ yellow pepper, de-seeded and diced
1 carrot, roughly chopped	2 tomatoes, diced
¼ cucumber, cut into small pieces	
½ red pepper, de-seeded and cut into small pieces	
juice of ½ lemon	
½ pint (300ml) V8 juice	
1 oz (25g) fresh basil	
couple of dashes tabasco (optional)	

1. Place all the main ingredients in a food processor and blend to a smooth consistency. Pour into a bowl, season and chill.

2. Garnish the soup with the very finely diced vegetables and an ice-cube.

Cook's tips:
Ideally make gazpacho with very ripe plum or beef tomatoes, as they are more authentic and often have more flavour. If not available, any ripe tomato will be fine.

V8 juice is a blend of tomato and vegetable juice. If it is not available tomato juice is adequate.

The appearance of this soup is vital and special care should be taken in the chopping of the vegetables for the garnish.

JAPANESE TOFU, MUSHROOM AND SNAP PEA SOUP

(Serves 2–3)

small quantity of sesame and olive oil	2 teaspoons rice vinegar
	1 dessertspoon tomato purée
1 onion, cut into quarters and sliced thinly	1 dessertspoon miso
2 sticks celery, thinly sliced	8 oz (225g) mushrooms, very thinly sliced
1 clove garlic, crushed	3 oz (75g) snap peas, sliced diagonally
½ oz (12g) root ginger, finely chopped	1 bunch spring onions, cut thinly on the diagonal
1 dessertspoon honey	9 oz (250g) plain firm tofu, drained and cut into cubes
2 dessertspoons soy sauce	
½ pint (300ml) dry sherry	a few beanshoots for garnish
1 pint (600ml) vegetable stock	

MARINADE FOR TOFU:

3 dessertspoons soy sauce

juice of ½ lime and ½ lemon

1 teaspoon honey

1 dessertspoon sesame oil

2 dessertspoons sherry

1. Preheat the oven to 400°F/200°C/Gas Mark 6. Prepare the marinade and mix in the tofu. Bake for 30 minutes, stirring a couple of times.

2. In a saucepan, fry the onion, garlic, ginger and celery in the oil mixture. Cook until soft. Add the honey, soy sauce, sherry, stock, rice vinegar, tomato purée and miso. Bring up to the boil then add the mushrooms, spring onions and snap peas. Cook until the mushrooms are soft.

3. Drain the tofu and stir it into the soup.

4. Season and serve with a garnish of beanshoots.

Cook's tips:
Miso is fermented soya beans. It is extremely nutritious and is excellent in stews and sauces as well as soups. It can be bought from most health food shops.

JERUSALEM ARTICHOKE AND ORANGE SOUP (v) (wf)

(Serves 4)

½ oz (12g) soya margarine	juice and zest of 2 oranges
1 onion, finely chopped	1¾ pints (1 litre) vegetable stock
1 stick celery, finely sliced	1lb 2 oz (500g) Jerusalem artichokes, peeled and chopped
1 large carrot, grated	
fresh thyme and rosemary, pulled off the stalk and finely chopped	vegan cream or yoghurt

1. In a large saucepan melt the margarine with the onion, celery, carrot and fresh herbs. Cook until soft.

2. Add the orange juice and zest plus the stock and the artichokes. Cook until the artichokes are soft.

3. Using an electric blender, process the soup until it is completely smooth. Season with salt and pepper.

4. Bring gently up to temperature then serve with a swirl of vegan cream or yoghurt.

Cook's tips:
Vegan cream and **yoghurt** are wonderful low calorie alternatives to the real thing and can be found in most health food stores.

LEMON DAHL SOUP (v) (wf)

(Serves 4)

2 oz (50g) fresh lemon grass	8 cardamom pods, roasted and ground
splash of oil	
1 red onion, finely chopped	juice of 1 lemon
2 carrots, grated	1½ pints (900ml) vegetable stock (including 8 fl oz (240ml) lemon grass stock)
1 stick celery, finely chopped	
1 clove garlic, crushed	2 oz (50g) red lentils
1 teaspoon ground cumin	3 oz (75g) green lentils
2 teaspoons ground coriander	2 dessertspoons tomato purée
1 teaspoon ground garam masala	3 oz (75g) coconut cream
2 teaspoons curry powder	1 oz (25g) fresh coriander
½ teaspoon aniseed, roasted and ground	

1. Place the lemon grass in a saucepan with 1 pint (600ml) of water. Bring to the boil and continue boiling until it has reduced by half. Drain, reserving the liquid (approximately 8 fl oz/240ml) and discard the lemon grass.

2. In a large saucepan cook the onion, carrots, celery and garlic in the oil with all the spices until soft.

3. Add all the remaining ingredients (except the fresh coriander) plus stock and cook gently until the lentils are soft. Using an electric blender, process the soup, keeping the texture fairly coarse.

4. Season with fresh coriander, salt and pepper. Bring gently up to temperature and serve.

Cook's tips:
This soup is exellent eaten with Naan bread or a sweet paratha.

MINESTRONE

(Serves 4)

2 tablespoons olive oil	1 x 14 oz (400g) can chopped tomatoes
1 onion, cut into quarters and thinly sliced	1 dessertspoon tomato purée
2 cloves garlic, crushed	1¼ pints (750ml) vegetable stock
1 carrot, diced	1 oz (25g) spaghetti, broken into short lengths
1 small potato, diced	1 oz (25g) fresh basil
2 oz (50g) broad beans	1 oz (25g) Parmesan cheese
1 oz (25g) French beans, cut into 1 inch pieces	salt and pepper
2 oz (50g) green cabbage, shredded	

1. Heat the oil in a large pan. Add the onion and garlic and cook until soft.

2. Add each of the vegetables, except the cabbage and broad beans.

3. Stir in the tomatoes, tomato purée and vegetable stock, bring up to the boil and cook for 10 minutes.

4. Add the cabbage leaves, spaghetti, broad beans, basil, Parmesan, salt and pepper. Simmer for approximately 10 minutes until all the vegetables and spaghetti are tender.

5. Serve with garlic bread.

MUSHROOM BISQUE

(Serves 4)

1 oz (25g) butter	2 dessertspoons soy sauce
1 onion, finely chopped	2 dessertspoons tomato purée
1 sprig rosemary, pulled off the stalk and finely chopped	1 lb (450g) mushrooms, thinly sliced
1 teaspoon paprika	1 large carrot, cut into very thin sticks
1 clove garlic, crushed	
½ pint (300ml) white wine	4 fl oz (120ml) single cream
2 fl oz (60ml) brandy	salt and pepper

1. In a large saucepan melt the butter then stir-fry the onion, rosemary, paprika and garlic until the mixture is soft.

2. Add the white wine, brandy, soy sauce and tomato purée. Bring to the boil, stir in the mushrooms and carrot and continue to cook until the carrot is soft. Reduce heat and slowly pour in the cream, taking care that the soup does not curdle. Season with salt and pepper and serve.

Cook's tips:
This is a fairly expensive soup to produce but for a special occasion it is well worth it.

PEA AND MINT SOUP

(Serves 4)

2 oz (50g) butter	1½ pints (900ml) vegetable stock
1 onion, finely chopped	1 lb (450g) frozen peas
1 clove garlic, crushed	fresh mint, pulled off the stalk (use a quantity to suit your taste)
few stalks of thyme, picked off the stalk and finely chopped	½ pint (300ml) single cream
2 dessertspoons white flour	

1. In a large saucepan melt the butter and fry the onion, garlic and thyme until soft.

2. Reduce the heat and stir in the flour. Cook until the texture of the roux changes.

3. Add the stock, peas and mint and gently bring up to the boil.

4. Using an electric blender, process until smooth. Finish with the cream, salt and pepper and garnish with mint leaves. Croutons are also excellent with the garnish.

Cook's tips:
This soup is an amazing verdant green. It is a wonderful summer soup and can be served hot or cold.

PUMPKIN, GINGER AND CARROT SOUP

(Serves 4)

1 oz (25g) butter	2 carrots, grated or finely chopped
1 onion, finely chopped	
3 sticks celery, thinly sliced	½ pint (300ml) milk
1 oz (25g) root ginger, finely chopped	½ pint (300ml) vegetable stock
	¼ pint (150ml) single cream
½ teaspoon ground nutmeg	1 oz (25g) fresh dill, finely chopped
1 clove garlic, crushed	
1 dessertspoon white flour	salt and pepper
1 lb (450g) pumpkin, peeled, de-seeded and cut into quarters	

1. Melt the butter in a saucepan and add the onion, celery, root ginger, garlic and nutmeg. Cook until soft (turn down the heat if the ginger begins to stick on the bottom of the pan).

2. Reduce the heat and stir in the flour. Cook for a few minutes until the texture changes.

3. Add the milk and stock plus the roughly chopped pumpkin and carrot. Cook until they are soft.

4. Add the cream and using an electric blender, process until smooth. Stir in the fresh dill, salt and pepper and serve.

Cook's tips:
Pumpkin has such a short season in England that it is great to really take advantage of it. However, English pumpkin can be rather bland so it is best to add other complementary vegetables to enhance the flavour.

RED PEPPER AND ALMOND SOUP (v)(wf)

(Serves 4)

olive oil	4 oz (100g) ground almonds
1 lb 8 oz (675g) red peppers, cored, de-seeded and cut in half	1 pint (600ml) vegetable stock
2 onions, finely chopped	salt, pepper and a splash of tamari
4 sticks celery, thinly sliced	1 oz (25g) fresh basil
2 cloves garlic, crushed	1 oz (25g) roasted, flaked almonds for garnish
2 teaspoons paprika	
2 x 14 oz (400g) tins of tomatoes	

1. Roast the peppers under a hot grill until they are lightly charred. Peel off the skin and discard.

2. Fry the onion, celery, garlic and paprika together with the olive oil for 5–10 minutes until soft.

3. Add the tomatoes, ground almonds and roasted peppers. Continue to cook for another 3–4 minutes. Add the stock and using an electric blender, process the soup until smooth.

4. Season with salt, pepper, a splash of tamari and finely chopped fresh basil.

5. Bring gently up to temperature and serve with a garnish of roasted almonds and fresh basil.

ROASTED AUBERGINE, RED PEPPER AND TOMATO SOUP (v)(wf)

(Serves 4)

1 aubergine, left whole	1 teaspoon paprika
2 red peppers, halved	3 heaped dessertspoons tomato purée
11 oz (300g) fresh tomatoes	
olive oil	1 pint (600ml) vegetable stock
1 onion, finely chopped	1 oz (25g) fresh basil
2 sticks celery, finely sliced	
1 clove garlic, crushed	

1. Preheat the oven to 400°F/200°C/Gas Mark 6.

2. Keeping the aubergine whole, brush with olive oil and stab with a fork about six times to allow the steam to escape. Place on a large baking sheet. Brush the pepper halves with olive oil. Place with the aubergine on the baking sheet. Place the whole tomatoes with salt, pepper and a drizzle of olive oil on the baking sheet with the peppers and aubergine.

3. Bake for approximately 30 minutes until tı e aubergine has collapsed in on itself, the peppers are slightly blackened and blistered and the tomato skins are broken and blistered.

4. Place the onion, celery, garlic and paprika in a saucepan with a little olive oil and cook until soft. Add the stock and tomato purée.

5. Cut the aubergine in half lengthways and using a spoon scoop out the flesh, discarding the skin. Add to the soup.

6. Carefully pull the seeds away from the peppers and peel away the skin, discarding both. Roughly chop the flesh and stir into the soup along with the roasted tomatoes.

7. Using an electric blender, process until smooth. Season with salt, pepper and finely chopped basil. Bring up to the boil and serve.

Cook's tips:
By roasting all the ingredients the flavours of the soup are greatly enhanced. The tomatoes, in particular, become beautifully sweet and any tartness that can sometimes occur with fresh tomatoes is completely removed. The soup has a special Mediterranean flavour to it and is wonderful eaten with crusty bread and lashings of olive pâté.

ROASTED AND SUNDRIED
TOMATO SOUP (v)(wf)

(Serves 4)

2 dessertspoons olive oil (from the sundried tomatoes)	2 medium-size red onions, diced
1 lb 6 oz (625g) ripe tomatoes	2 dessertspoons tomato purée
1 teaspoon paprika	1½ pints (900 ml) vegetable stock
3 large cloves garlic, kept in their skins	1 oz fresh basil
4 oz (100g) sundried tomatoes (see page 51)	salt and pepper

1. Preheat the oven to 375°F/180°C/Gas Mark 4.

2. Place the whole tomatoes and cloves of garlic on a baking sheet and sprinkle lightly with oil and salt. Roast for 45 minutes (giving them the occasional stir) or until the skins of the tomatoes are lightly blackened and the fruit has collapsed in on itself.

3. In the meantime, place the onions, paprika and oil from the sundried tomatoes in a saucepan. Cook until the onions are completely soft and starting to colour.

4. Stir in the roasted tomatoes and whole garlic (squeeze each clove out of its skin and discard the outer layer), plus any juices.

5. Add the stock, tomato purée and half of the sundried tomatoes. Using an electric food processor, blend until smooth.

6. Just before serving, thinly slice the remaining sundried tomatoes and stir them into the soup with the fresh basil and seasoning.

Cook's tips:
Garlic is truly wonderful when lightly brushed with olive oil and roasted in the oven. It becomes molten and very sweet. All the hotness that is present in uncooked garlic is totally removed. As a rule, the more garlic is chopped the more pungent it becomes. Roasting whole cloves of garlic gives a delicate flavour without the lingering smell on your breath.

SPANISH CHICKPEA SOUP (v)

(Serves 4)

4 oz (100g) chickpeas (soaked overnight, then simmered for about 1½ hours until soft. Drain thoroughly and rinse)	2 teaspoons ground cumin
	1 teaspoon dry mustard powder
	1 teaspoon white wine vinegar
olive oil	1 x 14 oz (400g) tin tomatoes
1 onion, finely sliced	1 pint (600ml) stock
1 stick celery, finely sliced	4 oz (100g) frozen peas
2 cloves garlic, crushed	1 oz (25g) fresh basil, chopped
1 teaspoon turmeric	

1. Heat the oil in a saucepan, with the onion, celery and garlic. Cook gently for 3–4 minutes.

2. Add the turmeric, ground cumin and dry mustard powder. Cook for a further 5 minutes to allow the spices to release their flavours.

3. Pour in the vinegar, stock, tomatoes and bring to the boil. Stir half of the chickpeas into the soup mixture and using an electric blender, process the soup leaving it a coarse consistency.

4. Add the remaining chickpeas, chopped basil and peas. Bring gently up to the boil, season and serve.

Cook's tips:
It is almost impossible to overcook chickpeas, however if they are under-cooked and quite hard they will cause stomach upsets. Always ensure that you soak them (preferably overnight) to avoid this.
  This is a hearty, substantial soup and is good served simply with crusty bread.

SPICED CAULIFLOWER AND POPPYSEED SOUP (v)(wf)

(Serves 4)

splash of oil	1 teaspoon paprika
1 onion, finely chopped	1 small cauliflower, cored, sliced into very small, thin pieces and divided into two
1 stick celery, sliced thinly	
1 clove garlic, crushed	
½ large green chilli, crushed	juice of ½ lemon
1 oz (25g) root ginger, finely chopped	1 dessertspoon sesame seeds, ground
1 teaspoon turmeric	2 dessertspoons poppyseeds, ground
2 teaspoons ground cumin	1 dessertspoon mango chutney
½ oz (12g) fresh coriander, finely chopped	1½ pints (900ml) vegetable stock

1. In a large saucepan, stir-fry the onion, garlic, ginger and celery with the oil and spices. Cook until the mixture is soft. (The ginger might stick to the bottom of the pan so add a little stock and it will lift off.)

2. Stir in the lemon juice, mango chutney, sesame seeds and poppyseeds plus half the cauliflower and stock. Continue to cook until the cauliflower is tender.

3. Using an electric blender, process the soup leaving the texture fairly coarse. Stir in the other half of the cauliflower and leave it so that it floats in the soup.

4. Bring up to temperature. Season with salt, pepper and fresh coriander. Serve.

SPINACH AND COCONUT SOUP ⓥ ⱳ

(Serves 4)

½ oz (12g) soya margarine	4 oz (100g) coconut cream, cut into chunks
½ teaspoon ground nutmeg	
1 onion, finely chopped	½ oz (12g) fresh dill, finely chopped
1 leek, finely sliced	
1 stick of celery, thinly sliced	
1½ pints (900ml) vegetable stock	
9 oz (250g) fresh spinach, any large stalks removed, and washed thoroughly	

1. In a saucepan melt the margarine with the onion, leek, celery and nutmeg. Cook until soft.

2. Add the stock plus coconut cream and continue cooking until the coconut cream has melted.

3. Having washed the spinach thoroughly add it to the ingredients in the saucepan and cook for a few minutes until the spinach is limp but bright in colour.

4. Using an electric blender, process the soup until smooth. Season with salt, pepper and fresh dill. Serve.

Cook's tips:
It is important not to overcook this soup. The colour needs to be a vibrant green rather than the sage green of overcooked spinach.

TOM YAM SOUP Ⓥ Ⓦ𝖿

(Serves 4)

SOUP:

splash of oil
1 red onion, finely chopped
1 clove garlic, crushed
1 oz (25g) root ginger, finely chopped
1 small red chilli, crushed
pinch of cinnamon and nutmeg
1 teaspoon ground cumin
1 teaspoon ground turmeric
2 pints (1.2 litres) stock (including special stock)
1 dessertspoon tamari
1 dessertspoon tomato purée
4 oz (100g) coconut cream
1 medium-sized sweet potato, diced
4 oz (100g) mushrooms, finely sliced
2 oz (50g) frozen peas
1 oz (25g) fresh coriander

STOCK:

¼ oz (6g) Kaffir lime leaves (dried or fresh), a few leaves kept back to float in the soup
1 oz (25g) dehydrated galanga
4 long stalks fresh lemon grass
4 oz (100g) tamarind block
2 pints (1.2 litres) water

1. Put the oil, garlic, ginger and chilli in a pestle and mortar until they form a paste. Place in a saucepan with the onion and all the spices. When soft add the stock, tamari, coconut cream and tomato purée. Bring gently to the boil, stirring occasionally to ensure that the coconut cream has melted.

2. Add the cubes of sweet potato, slices of mushroom and the reserved lime leaves. Cook gently for approximately 5 minutes until the potato is tender.

3. Stir in the frozen peas and coriander. Cook for a further few minutes to ensure the peas are tender and the coriander has released its flavour. Season to taste and serve.

Cook's tips:

All the ingredients for the special stock can be bought from oriental supermarkets or fresh from large supermarkets.

Kaffir lime leaves are dried lime leaves. It is wonderful to use fresh leaves which can be bought as part of a mixed packet including a small quantity of lemon grass, coriander and chillis. Lime leaves are particularly flavoursome when torn and left floating in a sauce or stock rather like a bayleaf.

Galanga is a root, similar in appearance and flavour to root ginger. If you are lucky enough to have a good oriental supermarket nearby it can be bought fresh, if not, in dehydrated thin slices.

Tamarind is a dried fruit derived from the tamarind tree. It has a sour taste and a very dark, sticky appearance. When using tamarind in a stock always drain it carefully through a sieve to remove stones.

Lemon grass is used especially in Indonesian, Thai and Indian cuisine. It can be bought fresh from large supermarkets or in larger quantities from oriental supermarkets. It can be frozen from fresh or can be bought dried or as a ground powder. A generous pinch of the latter is probably sufficient to flavour a dish for four people. If at all possible buy it fresh. Lemon grass has a beautiful flavour to it. The taste of lemon can be emphasised if the white of the root is chopped and ground and added to the soup or sauce. Break the stalks of lemon grass before adding to the stock so that the flavour is readily released.

TOMATO, GINGER AND ORANGE SOUP (v)(wf)

(Serves 4)

splash of olive oil	1 large carrot, grated
1 small onion, finely chopped	11 oz (300g) tomatoes, cut into quarters
1 small red onion, finely chopped	
2 cloves garlic, sliced	3 dessertspoons tomato purée
1 teaspoon paprika	¾ pint (450ml) orange juice
1 oz (25g) root ginger, grated and finely chopped	1 pint (600ml) vegetable stock
	salt and pepper

1. In a large saucepan, heat the oil then add the two different onions, garlic, paprika, root ginger and carrot. Cook for approximately 10 minutes until the onions are completely soft.

2. Stir in the tomatoes and continue to cook until they resemble a pulp.

3. Add the tomato purée, orange juice and stock. Remove from the heat and using an electric food processor, blend until completely smooth, making sure that the ginger has been totally puréed.

4. Return to the heat, season and gently bring up to the boil. Serve.

Cook's tips:
It is not necessary to peel root ginger. Like any other vegetable the goodness lies just beneath the skin, so by removing the skin some of the flavour and nutritional content is removed.

WATERCRESS SOUP (wf)

(Serves 4−6)

1 oz (25g) butter or soya margarine	2 sticks celery, thinly sliced
2 small leeks, dark green part trimmed off, and finely chopped	1 pint (600ml) vegetable stock
	1½ pints (900ml) milk
1 lb (450g) potatoes, cut into small chunks	5 oz (150g) packet of watercress
	double cream to garnish
½ teaspoon ground nutmeg	salt and pepper

1. Melt the butter or margarine in a saucepan. Add the leek, nutmeg, celery and potato and cook until soft. Stir in the stock and milk bringing gently to the boil.

2. Take the saucepan off the heat and add the watercress. Using an electric blender, process until smooth.

3. Return the soup to the saucepan and cook for a further 3−4 minutes.

4. Season with salt and pepper. Serve with a swirl of cream.

Cook's tips:
This soup is great served cold, especially in the summer.

It is important not to overcook watercress as it turns a horrible sage green and loses its flavour. Most of the flavour of watercress is in the stalk so make sure this part is not wasted.

Salads, Dressings and Dips

Rocket

Sorrel

Cos

oak leaf

Radicio

Rosso

chicory

Frisée

SALADS, DRESSINGS AND DIPS

Salads are wonderful dishes to create. With just a few ingredients — usually no more than four — attractive accompaniments to a main dish can be produced. Or, by combining pulses, grains, nuts, fruit or cheese with vegetables you will have a well-balanced and nutritious main course.

There are a few points to remember when creating salads, the most important being that they are only ever as good as the ingredients used: if the vegetables are raw they need to be of excellent quality — firm to the touch and vivid in colour.

A selection of good quality oils and vinegars is also essential. Olive oil is obligatory (the darker the colour green, the less refined and finer in taste) and sesame, walnut, peanut and coconut oils are also excellent, though they should be used sparingly as they are very strong. Both oils and vinegars can be infused with peppercorns, bay leaves, fresh chillis and large stems of rosemary, tarragon or parsley. These need to be left to infuse for at least two weeks before use. It is easy and quick to do and far more economical than buying them ready-made.

To create really tasty salad dressings which are also low in calories, the juice of limes, oranges, lemons, grapefruit and pineapple can be used. Raw vegetables and fresh herbs can also be added to a basic vinaigrette and blended, for example, spinach, watercress and tomatoes which will create dense colours and beautiful flavours. If a salad is made up of a lot of vegetables with a high water content, for example beanshoots, tomatoes and cucumber, be careful not to add too much salt or soy sauce as they draw out the juices from the vegetables. If using light, leafy vegetables, do not overdress them as they will go limp. Add the dressing just before serving.

Nuts are a great addition to salads, as well as being good providers of protein. To enhance their flavour, roast them in the oven until lightly golden in colour, then add a small quantity of soy sauce, paprika, chilli and crushed garlic. Toss together and roast for a few more minutes. As they cool the soy sauce and spices will stick to the nuts, completely transforming their flavour.

Like any dish, salads need to look attractive. The best way to achieve this is to combine cooked and raw vegetables, for example grilled peppers and onions, blanched broccoli, courgettes and French beans, and cauliflower and babycorn blanched in water to which a little turmeric has been added, turning them a vivid yellow colour. The use of seaweed (especially arame) adds a dramatic contrast of colour and taste, as does the use of fruit, either dried or fresh, cut into strips or sliced.

Salads, in conclusion, should be as vivid as you dare and the end result a rich fusion of colours, textures and tastes.

AUTUMN RED CABBAGE SALAD ⓥ⑩

(Serves 4)

1 oz (25g) butter or soya margarine	3 fl oz (90ml) red wine
1 small red cabbage, cored, cut into quarters and very thinly sliced	5 dessertspoons red wine vinegar
	½ teaspoon sugar
1 onion, cut in half and thinly sliced	3 oz (75g) raisins
1 pear, cored and cut into slices	GARNISH: chopped chives
½ teaspoon ground nutmeg	½ red pepper, de-seeded and cut into thin slices
½ teaspoon ground ginger	
½ teaspoon ground cinnamon	

1. Place the red cabbage in a colander and pour boiling water over it until the blue from the cabbage has virtually gone and the water runs clear. This removes any bitterness from the cabbage.

2. Place the onion, butter and spices in a saucepan and cook until tender. Add the cabbage and all the remaining ingredients. Cook on a low heat, covered, for 30 minutes, stirring occasionally.

3. Chill. Garnish with chives and the sliced pepper just before serving.

Cook's tips:
Red cabbage goes a very long way so take care when choosing the size! Small is beautiful for this recipe.
   The dish is equally good served cold as a salad or hot as an accompaniment to a main course.

BASMATI RICE AND LENTIL SALAD
WITH CURRIED MINT DRESSING (v) (wf)

(Serves 4–6)

8 oz (225g) brown basmati rice	**DRESSING:**
½ heaped teaspoon turmeric	juice of 1 lime
3 oz (75g) green lentils	4 dessertspoons olive oil
4 oz (100g) peas	1 dessertspoon tamari
4 oz (100g) fresh spinach, any large stalks removed, washed thoroughly and very thinly sliced	1 teaspoon curry powder
	1½ dessertspoons mango chutney
	½ oz (12g) (approximately) of mint leaves, pulled off the stalks

1. Place the basmati rice and turmeric in a saucepan. Add enough boiling water so that it comes 1 inch above the level of the rice. Bring to the boil, stirring occasionally, then cover the pan and allow the rice to simmer for approximately 20 minutes. As it reaches the end of its cooking time it is a good idea to allow the rice to steam by keeping the lid on the saucepan and turning the heat off. This prevents the rice from sticking to the base of the pan but do not stir the rice again from this point.

2. Put the lentils in a saucepan with cold water (no need to pre-soak them) and simmer for 20–25 minutes. Drain in a colander and rinse until the water runs clear.

3. Cook the peas in boiling salted water until tender. Drain.

4. Combine the rice with the lentils, peas and spinach.

5. Prepare the dressing by placing all the ingredients in a food processor and blending or by beating them together with a fork.

6. Thoroughly mix the dressing into the salad and chill.

Cook's tips:
By cooking the rice with **turmeric** the rice turns a wonderful yellow colour which is particularly attractive when used in salads.

Often when buying **lentils** (and chickpeas), small stones can appear mixed in with the pulse. These two pulses are particularly bad for finding 'foreign bodies' so to avoid a visit to the dentist, spend a couple of minutes picking through to check that it really is just pulses you are cooking!

BEETROOT AND FENNEL SALAD
WITH HORSERADISH DRESSING ⓥⓦⒻ

(Serves 4)

1 lb 2 oz (500g) cooked beetroot (without vinegar), grated	DRESSING:
small bulb of fennel, cut in half then sliced into long thin pieces	1½ dessertspoons ready-made horseradish
½ yellow pepper, de-seeded and cut into thin slices	2 dessertspoons white wine vinegar
fresh chervil or dill to garnish	1 dessertspoon olive oil

1. Place the vegetables in a large bowl and toss together.
2. Put the ingredients for the dressing in a screw-top jar and shake until they are well combined. Stir into the beetroot just before serving and garnish with chervil or dill.

Cook's tips:
It is advisable not to combine the vegetables too far in advance as the beetroot will colour everything and the vividness of the other vegetables will be lost.

CARIBBEAN GREEN BANANA SALAD

(Serves 4)

2 lbs (900g) green bananas	1 small fresh pineapple, peeled and cut into small cubes
juice of ½ lemon	
1 red onion, grated	1 oz (25g) fresh coriander, very finely chopped
3 sticks of celery, thinly sliced on the diagonal	
6 spring onions, sliced diagonally	½ quantity tofu mayonnaise (see page 64)

1. Peel and wash the bananas with the lemon juice. Cook in boiling salted water until tender, approximately 10−15 minutes. Drain and slice while still warm.

2. Add all the other ingredients to the bananas, stirring in the mayonnaise well so that the vegetables are completely coated. Serve on a bed of lettuce.

Cook's tips:
Green bananas are quite difficult to peel and it is often easier to use a knife to remove the skin.

Green bananas, unlike the popular yellow dessert variety, are not sweet, so the sweetness of the pineapple serves as a beautiful contrast.

CARROT, CELERIAC AND WALNUT SALAD

(Serves 6)

1 lb (450g) carrots, grated

1 bulb celeriac, peeled and grated

1 large ripe pear, cored and cut into thin slices

4 oz (100g) walnuts, roasted in the oven with soy sauce (see page 37)

4 oz (100g) vegetarian cheddar, cut into small cubes

1 quantity of tofu mayonnaise (see page 64)

1. In a large bowl combine the grated carrot and celeriac.

2. Stir in the walnuts, slices of pear and cheese.

3. Just before serving thoroughly mix in the mayonnaise.

CAULIFLOWER, PRUNE AND BANANA SALAD

(Serves 4)

6 oz (175g) dried prunes, stoned and chopped into small pieces

3 medium-sized bananas, sliced thickly and tossed with the juice of ½ lemon

½ medium-sized cauliflower, cut into florets and blanched in boiling water

½ quantity of tofu mayonnaise (see page 64)

bunch of chives to garnish

1. Toss the cauliflower with the bananas and chopped prunes.

2. Stir in the mayonnaise and garnish with chopped chives.

FRISSE AND FENNEL SALAD
WITH MEDITERRANEAN DRESSING (wf)

(Serves 4)

½ frisse lettuce (use a mixture of the inner and outer leaves so that there is a blend of colours)

12 oz (350g) tomatoes, sliced into quarters

1 chicory, cut in half and sliced on the diagonal

1 small fennel, cored, cut lengthways into quarters and sliced thinly on the diagonal

shavings of fresh Parmesan cheese and leaves of fresh basil to garnish

DRESSING:
2 dessertspoons olive oil

1 dessertspoon balsamic vinegar

juice of ½ orange

2 heaped teaspoons Chalice sundried tomato condiment

1. Toss all the vegetables for the salad together in a large bowl.

2. Place the ingredients for the dressing in a screw-top jar and shake until they are well combined.

3. Dress just before serving and, using a potato peeler, garnish with shavings of Parmesan cheese and leaves of fresh basil.

Cook's tips:
This salad really does have a wonderful feel of summer to it. It manages to capture the warm flavours and colours of a hot summer's day in the Mediterranean but is equally good eaten in Peckham!

GREEN CRACKED WHEAT SALAD

(Serves 4)

8 oz (225g) cracked wheat	DRESSING:
8 fl oz (240ml) boiling water	juice of ½ large lemon
7 oz (200g) fresh spinach, washed thoroughly and any large stalks removed	2 dessertspoons olive oil
	2 oz (50g) raw spinach
1 green pepper, cut in half, de-seeded and chopped into very small cubes	2 dessertspoons Chalice pesto
	2 dessertspoons Parmesan cheese, grated
3 spring onions, cut into 3 and thinly sliced lengthways	½ oz (12g) fresh coriander

1. Place the cracked wheat in a bowl and cover with the boiling water. Leave to stand for 30 minutes until soft and fluffy.

2. Meanwhile, put all the ingredients for the dressing in a food processor and blend until smooth. When the 30 minutes is complete, pour the dressing over the cracked wheat and mix thoroughly.

3. Place the spinach in a saucepan, without water, and cover with a lid. Cook for a couple of minutes until just limp and bright green. Drain and squeeze out any excess liquid.

4. Stir the spinach and green pepper into the cracked wheat.

5. Sprinkle the spring onions on top of the salad as a garnish. Chill, then serve.

Cook's tips:
Cracked (or bulgar) wheat is a semi-cooked wheat product and requires no cooking as such. As it is very bland on its own, I usually pour the minimum amount of boiling water over it so that it is fairly dry at the end of the 30 minutes and then add plenty of strongly flavoured dressing to give it the maximum amount of taste.

GREEN SALAD WITH AVOCADO
AND LIME DRESSING (wf)

(Serves 4)

2½ oz (60g) lambs lettuce	DRESSING:
8 oz (225g) broccoli, cut into small florets	juice and zest of 1 lime
3 sticks celery, cut thinly on the diagonal	1 medium-sized avocado, halved, stoned and the outer skin peeled away
1 × 14 oz (400g) tin artichoke hearts, rinsed, trimmed at the base and cut into quarters	3 dessertspoons sour cream
	1 dessertspoon olive oil
	salt and pepper

1. Blanch the broccoli florets in boiling salted water for 1 minute until bright green but still crisp. Drain.

2. Toss all the main ingredients together in a large bowl.

3. Place the ingredients for the dressing in a food blender and process until smooth.

4. Serve the dressing to the side or on top of the salad, but do not mix it in as it will spoil the colours of the dish.

Cook's tips:
Palm hearts are a good alternative to artichoke hearts and can be found tinned in large supermarkets. Unfortunately the process of removing the heart from the palm destroys the tree, which may, perhaps, affect your enjoyment of eating them.

LEEK AND PINE NUT SALAD
WITH A DILL AND DIJON DRESSING (wf)

(Serves 4)

12 oz (340g) small young leeks	DRESSING:
½ yellow pepper, de-seeded and sliced into thin strips	1 oz (25g) fresh dill, finely chopped
4½ oz (125g) button mushrooms, thinly sliced	1 teaspoon Dijon mustard
	1 teaspoon honey
3 oz (75g) watercress, with the stalks trimmed	juice of 1 lime
	1 dessertspoon olive oil
1½ oz (40g) pine nuts	salt and pepper
olive oil	

1. Trim the leeks, then, only using the white, cut into approximately 3 pieces. Cut each piece into long thin strips. Cook in boiling salted water for 3–4 minutes until tender. Drain and allow to cool.

2. Fry the pine nuts in a small quantity of olive oil until golden brown (this greatly enhances the flavour although they do smell a little fishy – extremely fishy if burnt). Drain on kitchen paper.

3. In a large bowl mix all the vegetables and pine nuts together.

4. To prepare the dressing beat the ingredients together with a fork. Dress the salad just before serving.

Cook's tips:
This is a fairly hearty salad and is ideal served as an accompaniment to a light main course or as a dish on its own.

LENTIL, TOMATO AND COTTAGE CHEESE SALAD

(Serves 4)

	DRESSING:
6 oz (175g) green lentils (no need to soak beforehand)	juice of ½ lemon
3 oz (75g) frozen peas	1 dessertspoon soy sauce
6 oz (175g) cottage cheese	1 dessertspoon olive oil
6 oz (175g) cherry tomatoes, halved	1 oz (25g) fresh coriander, finely chopped
	salt and pepper
	tabasco to taste

1. Cook the lentils for approximately 30 minutes until soft but not pulpy. Drain and rinse thoroughly until the water runs clear.

2. Toss the cooked lentils with the lemon juice, tabasco, soy sauce, olive oil, coriander and seasoning until well coated.

3. Cook the peas in boiling salted water until tender. Drain.

4. Combine the peas, cottage cheese and tomatoes with the flavoured lentils. Toss well, chill, then serve.

ORIENTAL BEANSHOOT SALAD
WITH ORANGE AND SESAME DRESSING (v)(wf)

(Serves 6)

1 lb (450g) beanshoots	**DRESSING:** juice of 1 orange
½ oz (12g) arame seaweed, soaked in boiling water	1 teaspoon sesame oil
1 orange pepper, de-seeded and cut into long thin strips	juice of ½ lemon
½ yellow pepper, de-seeded and cut into long thin strips	black pepper
6 spring onions, cut into diagonal slices (including the green of the onion)	
7 oz (200g) smoked tofu, cut into cubes	
4 oz (100g) mangetout, cut in half diagonally	

1. Drain the arame and squeeze out any excess liquid. Put all the salad ingredients in a bowl and mix thoroughly.

2. Place the ingredients for the dressing together in a cup and blend with a fork.

3. Dress the salad just before serving.

Cook's tips:

Beware! If you season beanshoots with salt or a highly seasoned product it draws the juices out of the beanshoots and they go limp very quickly.

Arame seaweed has a very delicate and slightly sweet flavour and grows in the seas around Japan. It can be bought from most health food shops.

Smoked tofu is a great way to eat what can be a very bland product. The tofu has undergone a smoking process that beautifully flavours the soya bean with a hickory taste. It is available from most supermarkets and health food shops.

PASTA AND ROASTED RED PEPPER SALAD WITH TOMATO DRESSING

(Serves 4)

8 oz (225g) penne pasta	DRESSING:
2 red peppers, halved and de-seeded	8 oz (225g) fresh tomatoes
	2 fl oz (60ml) olive oil
10 oz (275g) broccoli, cut into florets	juice of 1 lemon
	2 dessertspoons tomato purée
2 oz (50g) black olives, pitted	1 clove garlic
1 oz (25g) fresh basil, finely chopped	salt and pepper
1 oz (25g) fresh Parmesan shavings to garnish	

1. Cook the pasta in boiling salted water until *al dente*. Drain and rinse with cold water.

2. Drizzle some olive oil over the pepper halves and place under a hot grill until the skin blackens and blisters. Peel off the skin and discard. Thinly slice the flesh.

3. Cook the broccoli in boiling salted water for 1 minute until bright green in colour. Drain and rinse with cold water.

4. In a bowl combine the pasta, olives, peppers, basil and broccoli.

5. Place all the ingredients for the dressing in an electric liquidiser. Blend until smooth then combine with the pasta until well mixed.

6. Serve with a garnish of Parmesan cheese shavings.

Mint

Tarragon

Thyme

Sage

Lemon Grass

Chives

POTATO SALAD

2 lb 3 oz (1 kg) baby new potatoes

4 sticks of celery, sliced thinly on the diagonal

fresh mint, pulled off the stalk and finely chopped

1 quantity of tofu mayonnaise (see page 64)

1. Place the scrubbed (but not peeled) potatoes in a pan with half the mint and some salt. Bring up to the boil then simmer until tender. Drain and allow to cool completely.

2. Toss the potatoes with the celery and thoroughly combine with the mayonnaise. Garnish with remaining mint.

RATATOUILLE Ⓥ ⓦⓕ

(Serves 4)

olive oil	1 dessertspoon tomato purée
2 medium-sized aubergines, each one pricked with a fork about 6 times to allow the steam to escape and roasted whole	8 oz (225g) courgettes, sliced into rounds
	2 oz (50g) stuffed olives, halved
1 red onion, halved then thinly sliced	1 oz (25g) fresh basil, finely chopped
1 clove garlic, crushed	1 dessertspoon balsamic vinegar
	salt and pepper
1 lb (450g) tomatoes, each cut into 6 pieces	6 sundried tomatoes, cut into strips for garnish

1. Brush the aubergines with the olive oil and bake in a preheated oven at 400°F/200°C/Gas Mark 6 for approximately 30 minutes until they have collapsed in on themselves. When cool, slice lengthways and, using a metal spoon, scoop out the flesh. Roughly chop the flesh then leave to one side.

2. In a wok, stir-fry the onion and garlic with a little oil until soft. Stir in the tomatoes and tomato purée. Cook until it resembles a pulp.

3. Add the courgettes to the tomato mixture and cook until just tender.

4. Remove from the heat and stir in the aubergine flesh, olives and basil. Season with salt, pepper and balsamic vinegar. Chill, then serve with a garnish of sundried tomatoes.

Cook's tips:
This dish is delicious eaten cold as a salad or served hot and eaten with crusty bread or a jacket potato.

Sundried tomatoes can be very expensive if bought marinated but it's incredibly easy and much cheaper to marinate them yourself. Based on 4 oz(100g) of sundried tomatoes, first soak them in 4 fl oz (120ml) of water and 2 fl oz (60 ml) white wine vinegar for $1/2 - 1$ hour. Drain and rinse – this softens the tomatoes as well as removing the salt that is used in the drying process. Transfer the tomatoes to a jar with two cloves of sliced garlic, a few leaves of oregano, some peppercorns and enough olive oil (about 6 fl oz/150ml) to completely cover the tomatoes. Leave for twenty-four hours before using.

RED PASTA SALAD WITH SWEET ROASTED ONIONS AND FROMAGE FRAIS

This recipe was created by Jill Moss
who works as a chef at Food For Thought.

(Serves 4–6)

9 oz (250g) conchigliette (small pasta shells)	DRESSING: 6 oz (175g) fromage frais
1 small radicchio, cut into quarters, cored and thinly sliced	3 dessertspoons olive oil
	1 dessertspoon balsamic vinegar
5 small tomatoes, sliced into quarters, de-seeded, leaving just the skin (put the seeds to one side) then sliced very thinly	seeds and core of the tomatoes
	salt and pepper
2 red onions, cut in half, then the halves sliced into 3 chunks	
1 oz (25g) fresh basil, finely chopped for garnish	

1. Place the pasta in boiling salted water and cook for approximately 10–15 minutes, or until *al dente*. Drain and rinse with cold water.

2. Lightly brush the chunks of onion with oil and place under a hot grill. Roast for approximately 5 minutes until they start to blacken.

3. Toss the vegetables and pasta together.

4. Blend the fromage frais, olive oil, balsamic vinegar plus the offcuts of tomato with plenty of salt and pepper.

5. Mix thoroughly into the salad until well combined. Garnish with chopped basil and serve.

Cook's tips:
The fromage frais in the recipe can be substituted for ricotta or cottage cheese.

ROCKET, BROCCOLI, ROASTED RED PEPPER AND RED ONION SALAD (v)(wf)

(Serves 2–3)

olive oil	2 oz (50g) black olives, pitted and halved
2 red peppers, halved and brushed with olive oil	6 oz (175g) cherry mozzarella balls (if not available regular mozzarella cut into chunks)
2 red onions, halved, cut into thick chunks and brushed with olive oil	
	2 cloves garlic, crushed
1½ oz (30g) rocket (lambs lettuce is a good substitute if rocket is not available)	3 dessertspoons balsamic vinegar
	black pepper
13 oz (375g) broccoli, cut into florets	

1. Place the peppers and onion under a hot grill. Cook until the skins have blackened and started to blister. Leave to cool then carefully pull out the seeds of the pepper and gently pull off the skin, discarding both. Cut into long thin strips. Chop the onions into thick chunks.

2. Blanch the broccoli florets in boiling salted water until bright green in colour. Drain.

3. In a bowl mix all the vegetables together with the garlic, mozzarella and olives so that everything is well coated with the oil from the peppers and onion. Add the balsamic vinegar just before serving.

Cook's tips:
This dish can be served as a main course with crusty bread or as an accompaniment.

Balsamic vinegar is a sweet Italian vinegar aged in oak barrels. The better the vinegar, the thicker it is. I have tasted balsamic vinegar that has been matured for fifteen years and resembles treacle; the taste is heavenly and everything since has been a disappointment by comparison. I highly recommend that you buy the best you can afford as it is a great investment.

Rocket is related to the mustard family and the young leaves have a warm peppery flavour.

Lambs lettuce is now being used more extensively than ever, particularly as a salad leaf or lightly cooked, like spinach. Only the fresh young leaves are worth using. It is readily available in markets and most supermarkets.

ROCKET AND GORGONZOLA SALAD
WITH CROUTONS

(Serves 4)

olive oil	DRESSING:
2½ oz (60g) rocket or baby spinach leaves	juice of 1 lemon
5 oz (150g) white bread, thickly sliced, then cubed and made into croutons	black pepper
1 red pepper, de-seeded and halved	
5 oz (150g) gorgonzola, cubed	
1 dessertspoon Parmesan, grated	

1. Place the pepper halves under a hot grill and roast until the skin begins to blacken and blister. Discard the seeds and skin and slice the pepper into strips.

2. To make the croutons, trim the crusts off the bread and cut into cubes. Place on a baking tray with olive oil, salt and 1 dessertspoon of Parmesan cheese. Bake for 20 minutes in a preheated oven at 375°F/175°C/Gas Mark 4, turning occasionally until crisp and golden. Allow to cool before adding to the salad.

3. In a bowl toss the rocket (or spinach leaves), croutons, pepper and gorgonzola together. Dress with lemon juice and black pepper just before serving.

THREE RICE SALAD WITH COCONUT AND LIME DRESSING Ⓥ

(Serves 4)

2 oz (50g) brown rice (cooked with 1 dessertspoon of soy sauce)	4 oz (100g) French beans, topped, tailed and chopped into chunks
2 oz (50g) wild rice (cooked with 1 dessertspoon of soy sauce)	3 oz (75g) beansprouts
	1 oz (25g) sultanas
2 oz (50g) basmati rice (cooked with 1 teaspoon of turmeric)	2 oz (50g) coconut cream
	juice of 2 limes
4 oz (100g) whole cashews, roasted in the oven	salt and pepper

1. Cook the three different rices with their respective seasonings. When cooking the basmati rice add the coconut cream to the saucepan at the point when the rice is almost cooked. Stir until the coconut cream has melted. Turn the heat off and leave the rice with a lid on to steam until the rice is soft.

2. In a bowl combine the three different rices and stir in the lime juice, roasted cashews, salt and pepper.

3. Blanch the French beans in boiling salted water. Cook until they are bright green and crisp. Drain. Toss in with the other ingredients, chill and serve.

WARM SALAD WITH GORGONZOLA
AND GRAPEFRUIT VINAIGRETTE

(Serves 2–3)

6 spring onions, thinly sliced on the diagonal	**DRESSING:** juice of 1 grapefruit
8 oz (225g) chestnut mushrooms, sliced on the diagonal	2 dessertspoons olive oil
1 radicchio, ripped into chunks	2 dessertspoons white wine vinegar
1 chicory, cut thickly on the diagonal	1 teaspoon Dijon mustard
4 oz (100g) gorgonzola, cut into cubes	1 clove garlic, crushed
1 red pepper, halved	salt and pepper
fresh tarragon, pulled off the stalk	
iceberg lettuce for garnish	

1. Brush the pepper with oil and place under a hot grill until the skin blackens and blisters. Peel off and discard the skin and the seeds.

2. In a wok, gently warm all the ingredients for the dressing. Simmer until it has reduced in volume by approximately half.

3. To the concentrated dressing add the spring onions and mushrooms. Cook for a few seconds then add the radicchio, chicory and tarragon. Cook until the lettuces are just starting to go limp. Stir in the gorgonzola and slices of roasted red pepper.

4. Serve immediately on a bed of iceberg lettuce.

Cook's tips:
This is a beautiful recipe. The combination of melted cheese with crisp, warm vegetables with a hint of grapefruit is memorable. The secret is not to overcook the salad so that the crispness and colour are not lost (radicchio quickly loses its warm red colour and turns a horrible brown if cooked for too long). Unfortunately a salad such as this cannot be served at Food For Thought as it has to be cooked and eaten immediately, but I have served it at many catering functions, always with great success.

Chestnut mushrooms are readily available from supermarkets and have chocolate brown, rather than black, skins. They have more flavour than the regular field mushroom.

DRESSINGS

There are always jugs of salad dressings at Food For Thought that customers can liberally ladle over their already dressed salads. So delicious are they that I felt the salad section would not be complete without some of the more popular dressings. They are made very simply by blending all the ingredients in a food processor. Each dressing produces approximately six to eight servings.

BEETROOT AND HORSERADISH: (v) (wf)

6 dessertspoons olive oil

2 dessertspoons red wine vinegar

2 pre-cooked beetroot (not pickled)

2 teaspoons ready-made horseradish

small sprig fresh dill

salt and pepper

TAHINI AND YOGHURT:

1 heaped teaspoon light tahini

8 oz (225g) plain set yoghurt

2 dessertspoons olive oil

1 dessertspoon white wine vinegar

1 teaspoon ground cumin

juice of ½ lemon

dash of tabasco to taste

salt and pepper

TOMATO AND CORIANDER: (v) (wf)

2 fresh tomatoes

2 dessertspoons tomato purée

2 fl oz (60ml) white wine vinegar

4 fl oz (120ml) olive oil

1 teaspooon Dijon mustard

few leaves of coriander

tabasco to taste

salt and pepper

SPICY PEANUT: (v)

1 dessertspoon peanut butter

3 dessertspoons soy sauce

3 dessertspoons white wine vinegar

1 teaspoon dry mustard

8 dessertspoons olive oil

Rocket

Dill

Rosemary

Parsley

Chervil

Basil

DIPS

AUBERGINE AND FETA DIP

(Serves 4)

olive oil	2 dessertspoons lemon juice
2 medium-sized aubergines, kept whole and each one pricked about 6 times to allow the steam to escape	1 packet fresh mint, pulled off the stalk
	ground black pepper
1 clove garlic	
7 oz (200g) feta cheese	

1. Preheat the oven to 400°F/200°C/Gas Mark 6.

2. Brush the aubergines with some olive oil and place in the oven. Cook for approximately 30 minutes until they collapse in on themselves.

3. Leave to cool, then cut in half scooping out the flesh and discarding the skin.

4. Place the flesh in a food processor with the remaining ingredients. Blend until smooth.

5. Serve with crudités, tortilla chips or as a salad topping.

CHILLI BEAN DIP

(Serves 2−3)

3 oz (75g) red kidney beans, soaked overnight	½ oz (12g) fresh coriander
	½ large fresh chilli
1 teaspoon ground cumin	salt and pepper
1 dessertspoon tomato purée	paprika
5 fl oz (150ml) sour cream	

1. Cook the kidney beans for approximately 1 hour (making sure you boil them for the first 10 minutes). Drain and rinse.

2. Place the beans and all the other ingredients (except the coriander and paprika) in a food processor. Blend until smooth. Chill.

3. Garnish with a sprinkling of paprika and leaves of fresh coriander.

CHILLI DIP WITH FRIED PLANTAIN AND BREADFRUIT ⓥ ⓦⓕ

(Serves 2–3)

CHILLI DIP:
8 oz (225g) tomatoes, skinned and quartered

1 small red onion, finely chopped

1 large green chilli, finely chopped

1 heaped teaspoon tomato purée

1 clove garlic, crushed

splash of olive oil

oil for frying

VEGETABLES:
2 plantain

1 small piece breadfruit

1. Skin the tomatoes by sticking a fork into each one and holding into a gas flame until the skin pops and blisters. Peel off the skin and roughly chop. Place all the ingredients for the dip in a small saucepan and cook gently until they form a thick pulp. Leave to cool.

2. Peel the plantain and cut into thickish rounds. Soak in salted iced water for approximately 5 minutes as this prevents discolouration. Dry thoroughly with kitchen paper.

3. Cut the green skin off the breadfruit. Slice fairly thinly. Cook in salted water for 5–10 minutes. Dry with kitchen paper.

4. Place the breadfruit and plantain in very hot oil and fry (a wok is ideal for this), turning them over during the frying process until they are golden brown.

5. Drain on kitchen paper, sprinkle with salt, dip into the chilli dip and eat!

Cook's tips:
Plantain and breadfruit are both imported vegetables from the West Indies.

   Plantain should not be confused with green bananas. It looks like a large banana but should only ever be eaten cooked. The skin of the plantain should be yellow, just starting to blacken and soft to the touch, indicating that it is ripe and ready to eat.

   Breadfruit is becoming more popular and can be bought in pieces from any good street market. Buy in slices rather than a whole breadfruit as they can be very big.

GUACAMOLE ⓥ ⓦⓕ

(Serves 4)

5 oz (150g) tofu	½ fresh green chilli
1 avocado, halved, stoned and peeled	½ teaspoon paprika
	1 dessertspoon olive oil
juice of 1½ limes	2 tomatoes, quartered, de-seeded and sliced very thinly
juice of ½ lemon	
2 cloves garlic	salt and pepper

1. Drain the tofu of liquid and place in a blender. Purée until completely smooth.

2. Whilst keeping the blender going, gradually add in all the other ingredients, except the tomatoes. Process until the texture is no longer grainy.

3. Place in a bowl and stir in the thinly sliced tomatoes. Chill.

Cook's tips:
With the addition of tofu this recipe goes a lot further than traditional Guacamole. It is equally delicious as a dip, a salad topping or as a filling for jacket potatoes.

HUMMUS ⓥ ⓦⓕ

(Serves 5)

3 oz (75g) dried chickpeas, soaked overnight	3–4 fl oz (100ml) stock (water from the chickpeas)
juice of 1½ lemons	1 level teaspoon paprika
2½ dessertspoons light tahini	½ teaspoon ground cumin
2 cloves garlic	1 fl oz (30ml) olive oil
½ fresh green chilli	garnish of paprika and fresh coriander

1. After soaking the chickpeas overnight simmer for an hour until soft. Drain, reserving the liquid for stock.

2. Place all the ingredients, including the stock, in a food processor and blend until completely smooth.

3. Garnish with paprika and fresh coriander then serve with pitta bread, vegetable crudités or tortilla chips.

Cook's tips:
It is virtually impossible to overcook chickpeas. However, like any dried pulse, if you undercook them they can cause stomachache. Tinned chickpeas are reasonably good but drain and rinse them first.

ROASTED RED PEPPER AND ALMOND DIP (v)(wf)

(Serves 6)

olive oil	2 dessertspoons olive oil
2 red peppers, halved	½ teaspoon paprika
3 oz (75g) ground almonds	½ oz (12g) fresh basil
4 fl oz (120ml) tomato juice	3 cloves garlic

1.   Place the pepper halves under a hot grill with a drizzle of olive oil and cook until the skin starts to blacken and blister. Gently remove the skin and seeds, discarding both.

2.   Place all the ingredients including the roasted peppers in a food processor and blend until smooth.

3.   Season with salt and pepper.

TOFU MAYONNAISE

10 oz (275g) plain tofu	2 dessertspoons sour cream (or a mixture of sour cream and set yoghurt)
1 clove garlic	
1 teaspoon Dijon mustard	fresh herbs to taste (i.e. basil, dill, parsley)
1 dessertspoon white wine vinegar	
1 dessertspoon lemon juice	
2 fl oz (60ml) olive oil	

1.   Place the tofu in a food processor and blend to a smooth consistency (this will take a couple of minutes). Add the garlic, mustard, vinegar and lemon juice. Continue blending until well combined.

2.   Keeping the food processor going, slowly drizzle in the oil. Season with salt and pepper then stir in the fresh herb. If you wish the mayonnaise to be vegan stop here. If not, blend in the sour cream and yoghurt before stirring in the herb of your choice.

Cook's tips:
This recipe was developed at Food For Thought at the time of the controversy concerning the eating of raw eggs, which were thought to be carriers of salmonella poisoning. The mayonnaise is delicious and proved so popular that we have never reverted back to the traditional 'egg mayonnaise' recipe.

Main Courses

MAIN COURSES

Ask the average person to prepare a vegetarian main course and they will most likely be stumped, their imagination immediately deserting them and probably opting for pasta. Vegetarian food has come a long way since the days of the infamous nut roast, and now incorporates many fine ingredients from all over the world. The range of fruits and vegetables available from supermarkets and street markets is better now than it has ever been and combining these with the wonderful range of ingredients from Italy, India, China, Japan, Thailand and the West Indies, beautiful and appetising dishes are easily and quickly prepared.

There are a few points to remember when cooking vegetarian dishes, an important tip being to add flavours all the time, taking care not to confuse or overload the palate but to add flavours that compliment the dish. Always use fresh herbs, adding them (except for thyme and rosemary) at the end of the cooking process, so that the dish benefits from their full flavour. Dried herbs are a poor substitute and never add the same intensity of flavour or attractiveness as their fresh counterparts. Most, in fact, have been pushed to the back of the cupboard for six months yet are still expected to impart a wonderful taste and aroma.

The use of alcohol in cooking is another ready source of flavour. It can either be used to finish a sauce so that the full intensity of the liquor is appreciated, or added earlier in the cooking process, allowing it to burn off and the flavour to gently infuse the dish and, of course, your home!

Cheese is an obvious source of flavour and texture, ranging from the mild ricotta, mozzarella and cheddar to the richer Parmesan, goats cheese and feta, all of which benefit from being bought from a local delicatessen rather than pre-packed. If your local area has a Chinese supermarket, hunting along the shelves can reveal an Aladdin's cave of inspirational ingredients. Also take advantage of the local markets, trying, as much as possible, to use the vegetables in season, for example squash, marrow and pumpkin in October–November; leeks, turnips, Brussel sprouts and swedes in November–January; rhubarb, new potatoes and asparagus in the spring; broad beans, runner beans, beetroot, strawberries and blackberries during the summer.

As in all cookery, the appearance of the final dish is vital. Care should always be taken in the preparation of the vegetables so that the dish has a variety of shapes and colours to it and by varying the cooking processes, for example roasting, stir-frying and blanching, different textures are created within one dish.

Vegetarian cuisine should be a wonderful, varied and tasty way of eating, either as a way of life or as a pleasant alternative to meat or fish. In fact, it should be so good that even the heartiest carnivore can turn, if only every now and then, into a veggie convert!

BOMBAY CURRY WITH KOHLRABI AND BEETROOT (v)(wf)

(Serves 4–6)

SAUCE:

splash of oil

1 red onion, finely chopped

1 stick of celery, thinly sliced

1 oz (25g) root ginger, finely chopped

2 cloves garlic, crushed

2 heaped teaspoons tandoori spice

3 heaped teaspoons white sesame seeds

1 heaped teaspoon cumin seeds

3 heaped teaspoons fennel seeds

1 heaped teaspoon paprika

12 oz (350g) fresh tomatoes, cut into quarters

1 dessertspoon tomato purée

1 dessertspoon brown sugar

1 pint (600ml) vegetable stock

3 oz (75g) tamarind, combined with 1 pint (600ml) water brought to the boil and simmered for 20 minutes, then strained to produce 4 fl oz (120ml) stock

coriander leaves for garnish

VEGETABLES:

1 red pepper, halved, cored, de-seeded and sliced into long strips

1 medium cauliflower, cored and cut into florets

1 large sweet potato, cut into bite-sized pieces

1 kohlrabi, peeled and cut into small cubes

4 oz (100g) French beans, topped and tailed

6 oz (175g) cooked beetroot (without vinegar), coarsely grated

1. Place the onion, celery, ginger, garlic and spices in a large saucepan with the oil. Cook until soft.

2. Stir in the tomatoes, tomato purée and sugar. Cook until the mixture has become a pulp.

3. Add the strained tamarind stock plus vegetable stock and gently bring to the boil. Using an electric blender, process to a smooth consistency. Season with salt and pepper.

4. To prepare the vegetables: place the cubes of sweet potato in boiling salted water and cook until tender. Drain. Repeat with the cauliflower and French beans.

5. Lightly stir-fry the kohlrabi until it just begins to soften.

6. Combine the vegetables plus slices of pepper and beetroot with the sauce. Bring up to the boil and simmer for 3–4 minutes to allow the beetroot to 'bleed' into the sauce.

7. Garnish with coriander and serve with rice.

Cook's tips:

Beetroot is one of the most underrated vegetables. This is a superb and original way of cooking with it, allowing the sweetness to compliment the curried flavour. Beetroot also turns the dish a vibrant and rich red colour, creating a main focal point in a meal.

Kohlrabi is a beautiful vegetable in appearance (looking rather like a planet with sub-shoots coming out of the main part). It is pale green in colour and can be eaten raw or lightly cooked – if eaten cooked it is best to keep it quite crisp. It is available from large supermarkets and lends itself particularly well to a spicy dish.

BROCCOLI AND BABYCORN SWEET AND SOUR ⓥ ⓦⓕ

(Serves 4)

sesame or olive oil

1 onion, finely chopped

1 oz (25g) root ginger, finely chopped

1 clove garlic, crushed

6 dessertspoons tamari

12 fl oz (360ml) dry sherry

2 dessertspoons tomato purée

2 dessertspoons molasses

3 dessertspoons rice vinegar

8 fl oz (240ml) orange juice

juice of ½ lemon

2 dessertspoons cornflour

whole roasted almonds and slices of pineapple for garnish

VEGETABLES:

2 red peppers, halved, de-seeded and thinly sliced into strips

6 oz (175g) babycorn, halved diagonally

2 carrots, cut into small matchsticks

14 oz (400g) broccoli, cut into florets

4 oz (100g) sugar snap peas or mangetout

1. Roast the almonds (see page 37) ready for the garnish.

2. Heat the oil in a saucepan and add the onion, root ginger and garlic. Cook until soft. Add all the other ingredients, except the cornflour and lemon juice. Slowly bring to the boil.

3. Mix the cornflour with a little orange juice to make a paste. Drizzle into the boiling sauce, stirring constantly until it thickens. Season with salt and pepper. Stir in the slices of red pepper.

4. Bring a pan of salted water with the lemon juice in it to the boil. Add the carrots and cook until just soft. Drain.

5. Plunge the broccoli in boiling water so that it turns bright green. Drain. Repeat the process with the sugar snaps or mangetout. Drain. Repeat with the babycorn and cook until it is tender. Drain.

6. Add the sauce to the vegetables. Adjust seasoning if necessary and slowly bring up to temperature.

7. Serve on a bed of fresh Chinese noodles and garnish with roasted whole almonds and slices of pineapple.

Cook's tips:
The appearance of this dish is very important: the vegetables should be very lightly cooked so that they are quite crisp when eaten but have retained their colours. The finished dish should look fresh and bright with a variety of shaped vegetables.

BUTTERBEANS BAKED A LA NORMANDE

This dish was created and tested by Steve Wilcox, a Head Chef at Food
For Thought.

(Serves 4)

SAUCE:

2 oz (50g) margarine or butter	
1 small onion, finely chopped	
1 stick celery, thinly sliced	
1 small leek (white only), thinly sliced	
2 oz (50g) white flour	
¾ pint (450ml) vegetable stock	
¼ pint (150ml) dry cider	
¼ pint (150ml) single cream	
1 oz (12g) fresh tarragon, pulled off the stalk and chopped	
salt and pepper	

VEGETABLES:

4 oz (100g) dried butterbeans, soaked overnight, brought to the boil and simmered for 30–40 minutes, drained and rinsed.
2 oz (50g) margarine or butter
2 lb (900g) potatoes, cut into slices
8 oz (225g) carrots, cut into rounds
8 oz (225g) turnips, peeled and diced
8 oz (225g) swede, peeled and diced
8 oz (225g) leeks, sliced into rounds

1. Preheat oven to 375°F/180°C/Gas Mark 4.

2. For the sauce: in a large saucepan melt the margarine or butter then add the onion, celery and leek. Cook gently until the vegetables are soft. Stir in the flour to form a roux and cook until the texture changes to that of breadcrumbs.

3. Slowly add the stock and cider, stirring all the time so that no lumps form. Simmer gently for approximately 20 minutes, stirring regularly. Stir in the cream and tarragon. Season to taste.

4. For the vegetables: stir-fry the leeks and turnips together with some of the margarine or butter. Cook so that the vegetables still have some bite to them. Put to one side. Repeat this method with the carrots and swede.

5. Combine the vegetables and cooked butterbeans with the sauce. Adjust the seasoning if necessary. Turn into a suitably sized ovenproof dish.

6. Place the slices of potato in a large saucepan with cold salted water and par-boil so that they are still slightly crunchy. Drain and pat dry with kitchen paper. Layer on top of the vegetables. Melt the remaining margarine or butter and dab over the top of the potatoes.

7. Place the dish in the preheated oven and bake for 20 minutes until the potatoes are cooked. Finish by placing under a hot grill to allow the potatoes to go crisp and brown. Serve immediately.

CHARGRILLED MEDITERRANEAN VEGETABLES IN A ROASTED RED PEPPER SAUCE TOPPED WITH SPINACH SOUFFLE

(Serves 4)

SAUCE:
olive oil

2 red peppers, halved

1 onion, finely chopped

2 cloves garlic, sliced

2 sticks celery, thinly sliced

1 heaped teaspoon paprika

1 pint (600ml) vegetable stock

2 dessertspoons tomato purée

1 teaspoon Chalice pesto

1 oz (25g) fresh basil

salt and pepper

VEGETABLES:
olive oil

2 courgettes, cut into approximately three chunks then sliced lengthways

1 large aubergine, cut into rounds

small quantity of Chalice pesto

2 red onions, each cut into 6 segments

4½ oz (125g) button mushrooms, left whole

TOPPING:
9 oz (250g) spinach, stalks removed and washed thoroughly

pinch of nutmeg

2 eggs, separated

2 dessertspoons Parmesan cheese, grated

1. Preheat the oven to 375°F/180°C/Gas Mark 4.

2. Prepare the sauce by frying the onion, celery, garlic and paprika in a large saucepan with olive oil. Cook until soft.

3. Stir in the stock, tomato purée and pesto. Bring to the boil. Brush the peppers with oil and place under a hot grill until they blacken and blister. Discard the skin and seeds and add the flesh to the sauce. Using an electric blender, process until smooth then season with salt, pepper and basil.

4. In the meantime, brush the onions and courgettes liberally with oil. Brush each slice of aubergine with oil and a small amount of pesto. Place the vegetables under a hot grill until the flesh starts to blacken. Turn over, brush with oil and return to the grill.

5. Stir-fry the mushrooms.

6. Turn the vegetables into an ovenproof dish (a lasagne dish is ideal) then add the sauce.

7. Prepare the topping by cooking the spinach in a large saucepan with salt, pepper and nutmeg until limp. Squeeze out the excess juices. Place in a food processor with the egg yolks and blend until smooth.

8. In a separate bowl, using an electric whisk, beat the egg whites until they form soft peaks. Fold into the spinach mixture. Gently smooth over the top of the sauce and vegetable mixture.

9. Sprinkle with Parmesan cheese. Bake for 20 minutes until golden brown. Serve immediately.

CHICKPEA AND SPINACH KORMA

(Serves 4–6)

3 oz (75g) chickpeas, soaked overnight	VEGETABLES: 8 oz (225g) mushrooms, cut into quarters
splash of oil	
1 red onion, finely chopped	1 red pepper, cored and cut into squares
1 carrot, grated	9 oz (250g) fresh spinach, stalks removed, and washed thoroughly
1 oz (25g) root ginger, finely chopped	1 small cauliflower, cut into florets
3 teaspoons curry powder	2 large carrots, cut into rounds
1 teaspoon ground cumin	½ teaspoon turmeric
1 teaspoon garam masala	
1 pint (600ml) vegetable stock	TOPPING: 9 oz (250g) set yoghurt
1 dessertspoon tomato purée	
4 oz (100g) coconut cream	3 eggs
1 x 11 oz (300g) jar peanut butter	salt and pepper
juice of 1 lemon	½ oz (12g) fresh coriander to garnish
1 dessertspoon soy sauce	
1 dessertspoon honey	
1 oz (25g) fresh coriander	

1. Preheat the oven to 375°F/180°C/Gas Mark 4.

2. Place the chickpeas in a pan with plenty of water. Bring up to the boil then simmer for approximately 1 hour or until soft. Drain and rinse thoroughly.

3. Place the oil, onion, carrot, root ginger and all the spices in a saucepan. Cook gently until the mixture is soft.

4. Stir in the stock, tomato purée, coconut cream, peanut butter, lemon juice, soy sauce and honey. Slowly bring to the boil, stirring constantly, until the coconut cream and peanut butter have melted. Using an electric blender, process until smooth.

5. Season with fresh coriander, salt and pepper.

6. Add the mushrooms and the squares of red peppers to the sauce and allow them to cook slowly, so that all the juices released from the vegetables are contained in the sauce.

7. Cook the cauliflower and carrots in boiling salted water with the turmeric, to add colour, until just soft. Drain.

8. Cook the spinach very lightly in a covered saucepan until just limp. Drain.

9. Combine the sauce with the chickpeas and vegetables. Check the seasoning before turning out into a shallow dish.

10. For the topping, whisk the eggs, yoghurt, salt and pepper together until smooth. Stir in the coriander. Carefully ladle the mixture over the top of the vegetables until completely covered.

11. Bake for 20 minutes until the top is set and lightly brown in colour.

COUS COUS TOPPED WITH CHARGRILLED VEGETABLES

(Serves 3)

6 oz (175g) cous cous	COUS COUS SAUCE:
½ pint (300ml) boiling water	1 red onion, finely chopped
1 aubergine, cut into thin strips lengthways	1 clove garlic
1 large red pepper, halved	¼ pint (150ml) V8 juice
2 carrots, cut into thin strips lengthways	1 dessertspoon tomato purée
	1 dessertspoon Chalice pesto
1 clove garlic	a few drops tabasco sauce
olive oil	olive oil

SERVING SAUCE:	GARNISH:
10 oz (275g) fresh tomatoes, cut into quarters	2 oz (50g) black olives, pitted and sliced
1 red onion, roughly chopped	3 sundried tomatoes, cut into thin strips
½ red pepper, cored, de-seeded and roughly chopped	½ oz (12g) fresh basil, finely chopped
½ fresh green chilli, finely chopped	juice of ½ lemon

1. Place the cous cous in a bowl and cover with boiling water. Leave for 30 minutes until the water has been absorbed and it is light and fluffy. (Don't worry if it seems dry as the sauce will moisten it later.) Leave to one side.

2. For the cous cous sauce: fry the onion and garlic in a little olive oil until soft (approximately 4 minutes). Add the remaining ingredients. Cook for a few minutes before thoroughly stirring into the fluffy cous cous.

3. For the serving sauce: place the chilli, onion, red pepper and fresh tomatoes in a saucepan. Cook until the tomatoes resemble a pulp. Using an electric blender, process the sauce until thick and smooth. Season to taste.

4. Preheat the grill.

5. Carefully prepare all the vegetables, cutting the aubergine and carrots lengthways. Liberally brush with olive oil and rub with a clove of garlic.

6. Place the vegetables under a hot grill and roast on each side until the skin just starts to blacken. (Remember to brush the vegetables with oil on both sides.)

7. Discard the seeds and skin of the pepper and chop the flesh into large squares. Place together with the aubergine and carrots on the flavoured cous cous in a serving dish. Immediately sprinkle with a garnish of olives, sundried tomatoes, fresh basil and lemon juice. Serve the sauce to the side.

FONDUE

(Serves 4)

1 oz (25g) butter	**SUGGESTED VEGETABLES FOR DIPPING:**
2 cloves garlic, crushed	sugar snap peas
1 onion, finely chopped	cooked potato cubes
2 teaspoons mustard powder	red or green pepper cut into strips
6 oz (175g) emmenthal cheese, grated	blanched broccoli and cauliflower
6 oz (175g) gruyère cheese, grated	cubes of bread
6 fl oz (180ml) milk	
¾ pint (450ml) stock	
3 fl oz (90ml) kirsch	
3 dessertspoons cornflour	
salt and pepper	

1. In a saucepan melt the butter then add the onion and garlic. Cook until soft but not discoloured. Add the mustard powder, milk and stock then stir in the emmenthal and gruyère. Cook gently, stirring all the time until the cheese has melted. Blend until the sauce is smooth.

2. Place the kirsch and cornflour in a cup and mix into a smooth paste.

3. Bring the sauce up to the boil then drizzle in the cornflour mixture, stirring constantly. Cook for a further couple of minutes to cook the cornflour. The sauce should be a thick, coating consistency. Season to taste.

4. Use whatever means available to keep the sauce hot while the vegetables and/or bread are dipped in (see below). Almost any vegetable is suitable for dipping but it is preferable to cook or blanch them first, depending on the variety. Kebab sticks or skewers are ideal to use for dipping the vegetables in the sauce.

Cook's tips:
Fondues seem to have slipped out of fashion but they are a good, sociable way to eat with a few friends, although the 'stringy' consistency of the cheeses can make for a messy evening!

If you do not possess a fondue set, a cheaper option is a small pot stand with a hole in the bottom where night candles can fit. When they are lit they will keep the fondue warm perfectly. These are available from most department stores and good kitchen shops.

GADO GADO ⓥ ⓦⓕ

(Serves 4–5)

SAUCE:
splash of oil (peanut oil if available)

1 onion, finely chopped

1 stick celery, thinly sliced

1 oz (25g) root ginger, finely chopped

½ large green chilli, finely chopped

1 clove garlic, crushed

1 dessertspoon ground sesame seeds

1 dessertspoon tamari or soy sauce

1 dessertspoon tomato purée

1 dessertspoon molasses

1 × 11 oz (300g) jar peanut butter

1 pint (600ml) stock

juice of 1 lemon

1 oz (25g) fresh coriander, finely chopped

VEGETABLES:
3 carrots, sliced into rounds

1 small cauliflower, cut into florets

1 lb (450g) fresh egg or rice noodles (pre-cooked)

2 courgettes, sliced lengthways in half and then cut into half circles

4 oz (100g) babycorn, sliced diagonally in half

1. For the sauce: place the oil, onion, celery, root ginger, chilli, garlic and sesame seeds in a saucepan. Cook until mixture is soft.

2. Add all the remaining sauce ingredients (except the fresh coriander) and cook gently, stirring all the time until the peanut butter has melted and the sauce has slowly come to the boil. Stir in the coriander and season to taste.

3. For the vegetables: cook the cauliflower, carrots and babycorn together in boiling salted water. Drain then stir into the sauce.

4. Stir-fry the courgettes with a little salt (and coriander if you desire). Drain and stir into the sauce.

5. Stir in the noodles (pre-cooked according to packet instructions if not fresh) and bring the Gado Gado up to the boil. Serve.

Cook's tips:

This dish is really a meal in itself and does not need to be served with anything other than perhaps a light accompanying salad.

As the sauce of Gado Gado is predominantly peanut butter its success depends largely on the quality of peanut butter used.

Fresh, thick **egg noodles** are best for this dish and are bought pre-cooked. A vegan alternative are white rice noodles. Dried noodles can be used (these will need pre-cooking, before adding to the dish) but the thick ones are preferable as they do not disintegrate.

GOATS CHEESE AND AUBERGINE CROSTINI

(Serves 2)

olive oil

1 small aubergine, cut into rounds

small quantity of Chalice sundried tomato paste

4 oz (100g) firm goats cheese, cut into slices

1 small baguette, sliced on the slant into oval pieces

1 clove garlic, whole

few leaves of fresh basil

GARNISH
pinch of paprika

few radicchio leaves

½ red pepper, de-seeded and thinly sliced

few black olives

small quantity of olive oil

1. Brush each slice of aubergine with oil then spread over a small quantity of sundried tomato sauce. Place under a hot grill, and when golden brown, flip over and brush again with oil.

2. Rub the whole clove of garlic over each slice of baguette and brush lightly with oil. Toast on both sides until golden.

3. On each piece of baguette place a slice of aubergine and on top of that a slice of goats cheese.

4. Return to the grill until the cheese starts to melt and bubble.

5. Serve immediately with a sprinkling of paprika, chopped basil and a side salad of radicchio leaves, thin slices of red pepper, black olives and a drizzle of olive oil. This dish is perfect as a light summer main course.

ITALIAN AUBERGINE AND MOZZARELLA LAYER

(Serves 4)

	TOMATO SAUCE:
olive oil	1 onion, finely chopped
1 large aubergine, cut into rounds	1 clove garlic, crushed
12 oz (350g) potatoes, cut into thin rounds	12 oz (350g) fresh tomatoes, skinned and cut into quarters
6 fl oz (180ml) milk	2 fl oz (60ml) red wine
4½ oz (125g) mozzarella cheese, grated	2 fl oz (60ml) V8 juice
1 oz (25g) fresh Parmesan, grated to garnish	1 dessertspoon tomato purée
	1 dessertspoon Chalice pesto
	½ oz (12g) fresh basil, finely chopped

1. Preheat oven to 375°F/180°C/Gas Mark 4.

2. Prepare the aubergine (see below). Dry on kitchen roll.

3. Place the potatoes in an ovenproof dish with the milk and bake for 20 minutes until just cooked.

4. Fry the aubergine in olive oil until soft and lightly golden. Drain on kitchen paper.

5. For the sauce: fry the onion and garlic until soft, add all other ingredients except the basil and cook for a further 10 minutes until the sauce is fairly smooth. Stir in the basil and season to taste.

6. In an ovenproof dish layer the ingredients in the following order: tomato sauce, aubergine, potato, mozzarella, then repeat once more finishing with the mozzarella. Bake for 20 minutes until lightly golden.

7. Garnish with Parmesan cheese and serve immediately.

Cook's tips:

Aubergine is a very acidic vegetable and it was generally believed that the bitter juices should be removed before cooking. The best way to do this is to wash the whole aubergine before it has been cut. Then trim off the end and cut into rounds or cubes. Sprinkle with salt and leave for approximately 10–15 minutes so that the salt draws out the juices. Rinse under cold water andsqueeze the excess moisture out of the aubergine. This is an essential part of the process as aubergine is very absorbent. The aubergine is now ready to cook. However, this process really is only necessary if the aubergine is soft to the touch. If the skin is bright and shiny and the vegetable firm to the touch, then there is no need to go through the process of salting.

MEXICAN STEW WITH A TOMATO AND LIME SAUCE (v)(wf)

(Serves 4)

SAUCE:

olive oil

½ onion, finely chopped

1 small red chilli, finely chopped

3 cloves garlic, crushed

3 sticks celery, finely chopped

¼ teaspoon ground nutmeg

¼ teaspoon ground cinnamon

2 teaspoons paprika

3 teaspoons ground coriander

8 oz (225g) tomatoes, skinned and cut into quarters

1 dessertspoon tomato purée

¾ pint (450ml) tomato juice

juice of 1½ limes

3 heaped teaspoons lime pickle

1 dessertspoon tamari or soy sauce

1 oz (25g) fresh coriander, finely chopped

salt and pepper

VEGETABLES:

½ cauliflower, cut into florets

1 lb (450g) sweet potato, cut into bite-size pieces

6 oz (175g) frozen peas

9 oz (250g) fresh spinach, stalks removed, and washed thoroughly

pinch of nutmeg

GARNISH:

½ lime cut into thin slices

½ avocado, sliced

handful of spicy tortilla chips

1. Fry the onion, garlic, chilli and celery with the oil and all the spices. Cook for 5 minutes until soft.

2. Add the tomatoes and tomato purée. Continue cooking until the mixture is a pulp. Add the tomato juice and the lime juice and lime pickle. Cook for a further couple of minutes. Stir in the tamari, fresh coriander and seasoning.

3. Cook the cauliflower in boiling, salted water until just tender. Drain, reserving the water.

4. Add the potatoes (there is no need to peel them) to the same water and cook until soft. (Sweet potatoes cook quicker than regular potatoes.)

5. Cook the spinach with a little nutmeg, salt and pepper in a saucepan (no water is required) until just limp. Drain.

6. Add the sauce to the vegetables and peas (no need to cook the peas in advance). Cook for a further 5 minutes so that the whole dish is hot.

7. Garnish with thin slices of lime, avocado and tortilla chips. This dish is excellent accompanied with rice.

Cook's tips:

Limes are becoming increasingly popular. A very simple way of using them is to bake a sweet potato in its jacket and eat it plain with just salt, lime juice and some chopped chilli – if you have the nerve!

MOUSSAKA

(Serves 6)

TOMATO SAUCE:

olive oil

1 onion, finely chopped

2 cloves garlic, crushed

2 sticks celery, thinly sliced

1 small carrot, grated

2 × 14 oz (400g) tins chopped tomatoes

2 dessertspoons tomato purée

splash of soy sauce

1 oz (25g) fresh basil, finely chopped

WHITE SAUCE:

2 oz (50g) butter

2 dessertspoons white flour

pinch of nutmeg

¼ pint (150ml) milk

4 oz (100g) vegetarian cheddar cheese, grated

1 egg white, beaten until stiff

VEGETABLES:

4 oz (100g) green lentils

1½ lb (675g) potatoes, cooked whole then sliced

2 aubergines, sliced into rounds

10 oz (275g) mushrooms, cut into quarters

1 red pepper, cored, de-seeded and sliced into thin strips

1 lb (450g) spinach, stalks removed and washed thoroughly

1. Preheat the oven to 375°F/180°C/Gas Mark 4.

2. Place the lentils in a large saucepan and cook until tender (approximately 15 minutes). Drain in a colander and rinse until the water runs clear.

3. Place the slices of aubergine on a baking tray with plenty of olive oil. Roast in the preheated oven for 20 minutes until tender, turning occasionally.

4. Stir-fry the mushrooms and peppers together in a wok. Set aside, retaining any juices released by the vegetables.

5. Cook the spinach in a saucepan until bright green and limp. No liquid is required. Squeeze out any excess juices and finely chop.

6. In a large saucepan fry the onion, garlic, celery and carrot with the olive oil until soft. Add the tomatoes, tomato purée and soy sauce. Bring up to the boil and season with fresh basil, salt and pepper (the sauce can either be blended or left coarse). Set the tomato sauce to one side.

7. In a small pan melt the butter with the nutmeg. Lower the heat and stir in the flour. Cook until the texture of the roux changes to that of breadcrumbs. Slowly add the milk, stirring all the time so that no lumps form. Stir in the cheese and season with salt and pepper. Continue to cook until the cheese has melted.

8. In a separate bowl fold the beaten egg whites into the cheese sauce.

9. Combine the tomato sauce with the lentils, mushrooms, peppers and spinach. Cover a deep dish with half of the tomato mixture, then layer half the aubergines on top. Layer half the sliced potatoes on top of the aubergines. Repeat, covering the final layer of potatoes with cheese sauce.

10. Sprinkle with Parmesan cheese and bake in the preheated oven for 20–30 minutes until golden brown on top and bubbling. Serve immediately with a crisp salad.

Cook's tips:
To give the aubergines even more flavour, spread a small quantity of pesto sauce over each slice, then roast with olive oil in the oven until tender (approximately 20 minutes).

There are many parts to this dish but it doesn't have to be time-consuming. Be systematic and prepare everything first – the dish is well worth it.

MUSHROOMS STUFFED WITH AUBERGINE PUREE ⓦⓕ

(Serves 4 as a main course, 8 as a starter)

8 large field mushrooms	2 dessertspoons light tahini
2 aubergines kept whole	dash of tabasco (optional)
1 clove garlic	1 oz (25g) fresh coriander
juice of ½ lemon	salt and pepper
5 oz (150g) natural yoghurt	

1. Preheat oven to 400°F/200°C/Gas Mark 6.

2. Wash the aubergines. With a fork, prick each one about six times to allow the steam to escape and brush with oil. Place on a baking tray in the oven and cook for 35 minutes until soft and collapsing in on themselves.

3. Cut the stalks of the mushrooms off at the base and discard. Place them 'bottoms up' on a baking tray. Brush with oil and lightly sprinkle with salt and pepper. Place in the oven and cook for 5−10 minutes so that they are still firm. Cool on a wire tray.

4. Cut the roasted aubergines in half and using a spoon gently scoop out the flesh, discarding the skin. Place in a food processor with the garlic, lemon juice, yoghurt, tahini, coriander and tabasco. Blend until a smooth consistency and season with salt and pepper.

5. Generously heap the aubergine purée into each of the mushrooms. Chill. Serve on a bed of lambs lettuce and radicchio as a starter or as a main course.

Cook's tips:
Field mushrooms are the large, very black variety of mushroom that seem to have been designed especially for filling with various delicious-concoctions.

MUSHROOMS STUFFED WITH LEEK, WATERCRESS AND PESTO

(Serves 4 as a main course, 8 as a starter)

8 large field mushrooms (see page 88)	3 heaped teaspoons Chalice pesto
1 oz (25g) butter	pinch of nutmeg
1 lb (450g) leeks, thinly sliced	1 dessertspoon lemon juice
3 oz (75g) watercress, washed	salt and pepper

1. Plunge the mushrooms into boiling salted water until just starting to go soft (no more than 2 minutes). Drain on a triple layer of kitchen paper, bottom side up.

2. Stir-fry the leeks and nutmeg in butter until soft. Add the watercress until soft and limp (this will only take a few seconds). Blend in a food processor with the lemon juice, pesto, salt and pepper.

3. Generously fill each mushroom with the leek and watercress purée. Chill then serve on a bed of lambs lettuce.

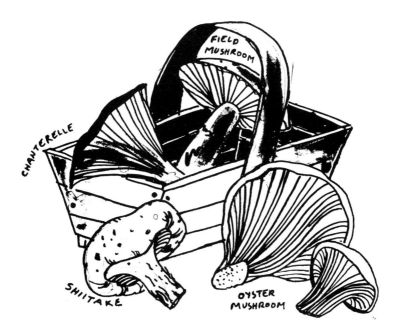

NEW ORLEANS GUMBO (v) (wf)

This recipe was adapted and tested by Steve Wilcox,
a Head Chef at Food For Thought.

(Serves 4—6)

4 oz (100g) dried black-eyed beans (soaked overnight then simmered for 20—30 minutes, drained and rinsed thoroughly)	4 oz (100g) okra, tops trimmed
	1 × 7 oz (200g) tin sweetcorn, drained
oil	1 × 14 oz (400g) tin chopped tomatoes
1 onion, finely chopped	5 dessertspoons tamari or soy sauce
2 cloves garlic, crushed	
½ oz (12g) fresh root ginger, finely chopped	3 dessertspoons tomato purée
	5 dessertspoons molasses
1 or 2 fresh green chillis, finely chopped	3 dessertspoons white wine vinegar
1 small aubergine, diced	¾ pint (450ml) vegetable stock
1 sweet potato, scrubbed and diced	2 dessertspoons cornstarch (mixed with a little cold water to form a paste)
1 red pepper, halved, cored, de-seeded and sliced into cubes	chopped spring onions and fresh coriander for garnish
1 green pepper, halved, cored, de-seeded and sliced into cubes	
2 courgettes, cut into rounds	

1. Place the onion, garlic, ginger and fresh chillis with the oil in a large saucepan and cook until tender.

2. Add the cubed aubergine and sweet potato. Continue to cook for a few minutes, stirring all the time to prevent sticking.

3. Add the remaining ingredients (except the black-eyed beans and cornstarch) and gently simmer for 30—40 minutes, stirring occasionally until all the vegetables are tender.

4. Thicken the stew by drizzling the cornstarch into the mixture, stirring all the time. Add the black-eyed beans and simmer for a further 10 minutes. Season and garnish with chopped spring onions and fresh coriander. Serve with hunks of bread.

ORIENTAL NOODLES (wf)

(Serves 2–3)

SAUCE:

sesame oil and olive oil

1 onion, cut in quarters and thinly sliced

1 oz (25g) root ginger, chopped finely

1 dessertspoon sesame seeds, ground

3 dessertspoons soy sauce

juice of 1 orange

¼ oz (6g) dried blackbeans

2 dessertspoons plum sauce

1 dessertspoon rice vinegar

1 dessertspoon honey

1 dessertspoon tomato purée

4 fl oz (120ml) stock

2 fl oz dry sherry

1 dessertspoon cornflour (mixed with a very small quantity of water or sherry)

VEGETABLES AND ACCOMPANIMENTS:

1 red pepper, halved, de-seeded and sliced into thin strips

8 oz (225g) egg noodles, pre-cooked (fresh, fairly large noodles are the best)

8 oz (225g) broccoli, cut into small florets

2 oz (50g) whole cashew nuts, roasted in the oven with a dash of tamari

1. Place the two oils (it is better to use a mixture as sesame oil is very strong), onion, root ginger and sesame seeds in a saucepan. Cook until the onion is soft.

2. Add all the remaining ingredients including the stock and dry sherry and gently bring to the boil. Mix the cornflour with a little sherry or water and slowly pour into the boiling sauce, stirring all the time (the cornflour not only thickens the sauce but also gives it an attractive glossiness).

3. Add the red pepper and noodles to the sauce.

4. Place the broccoli in boiling salted water for 1 minute until bright green but still very crisp. Drain and stir into the sauce. Season with salt and pepper.

5. Garnish with the roasted cashew nuts and serve immediately.

Cook's tips:

Most of the ingredients listed in this recipe are now stocked in super-markets but if you have a local Chinese supermarket you will have absolutely no problem.

Plum sauce is made from a blend of sugar, sweet potato, rice vinegar and plum purée. Blackbeans are the dried variety, very small in size and salty. They should not be confused with black kidney beans.

ORIENTAL PANCAKES
WITH SAKE AND ORANGE SAUCE

(Makes 6 large or 12 small pancakes)

BATTER:

4 oz (100g) white flour

½ teaspoon salt

2 eggs

5 fl oz (150ml) milk

5 fl oz (150ml) water

2 dessertspoons sunflower oil

chopped chives

FILLING:

1 red pepper, cored, de-seeded then sliced into fine strips

6 oz (175g) mushrooms, sliced very thinly

4 spring onions, sliced into 1 inch strips

2 oz (50g) mangetout, cut in half diagonally

7 oz (200g) beanshoots

SAUCE:

1 oz (25g) root ginger, finely chopped

½ large green chilli, finely chopped

2 cloves garlic, sliced

splash of oil

½ pint (300ml) *sake* (available from Chinese stores)

¼ pint (150ml) orange juice

2 dessertspoons soy sauce

2 dessertspoons honey

1 dessertspoon rice vinegar

2 level dessertspoons cornflour

1. For the batter: place the dry ingredients in a large bowl. Make a well in the centre and crack the eggs into it. Beat, then slowly add the milk, water and oil, whisking well between each addition to avoid lumps. Stir in the chives and refrigerate.

2. For the sauce: finely chop the garlic, chilli and root ginger and grind together in a pestle and mortar until it becomes a paste. Set one third aside.

3. Heat the oil in a saucepan and fry the ginger paste until the aroma of the three ingredients is released. Add the *sake*, orange juice, soy sauce, honey and rice vinegar.

4. Bring to the boil and continue to boil for 10 minutes. This burns off the alcohol and also gives a far more concentrated flavour to the sauce.

5. Combine the cornflour with a tiny amount of orange juice to form a paste. Drizzle into the sauce, stirring all the time, until it has a glossy appearance (approximately 30 seconds). Season if necessary.

6. For the filling: prepare all the vegetables. It is worth taking the time to slice the ingredients thinly and attractively, making sure the vegetables are small enough so they don't break the pancake when filled.

7. Heat the oil in a wok until very hot. Fry the remaining third of the ginger, garlic and chilli mixture then add in the remaining vegetables (except the beanshoots). Cook until the vegetables are bright in colour (1 minute approximately).

8. Stir in the beanshoots plus 2 dessertspoons of sauce plus black pepper. Cook the beanshoots until they are just going soft.

9. Cook off the pancakes (see cook's tips).

10. Place the best side of the pancake down. Divide the filling into six portions and place one portion at the nearest end of the pancake. Fold over the nearest end, then each of the sides. Roll the pancake up and place seam side down on a lightly greased baking tray. Repeat the process for the other pancakes.

11. Cover the baking tray with foil and place in a hot oven (425°F/225°C/Gas Mark 7) for 10 minutes until the pancakes are warmed through.

12. Serve the pancakes on top of the *sake* sauce.

Cook's tips:

Batter is basically a rather bland mix of ingredients so it is always good to add something to either add flavour or enhance the appearance. Beer, fruit juice, any fresh herb or spice or flaked almonds are a few good examples.

The secret to successful pancake making is to have a good pan, preferably with a very small edge or no edge at all. Always keep the pan hot and oiled between pancakes and use a palette knife to ease the pancake over onto its other side.

Sake is a Japanese drink with a very high alcohol content. It can be drunk either hot or cold and is made from rice.

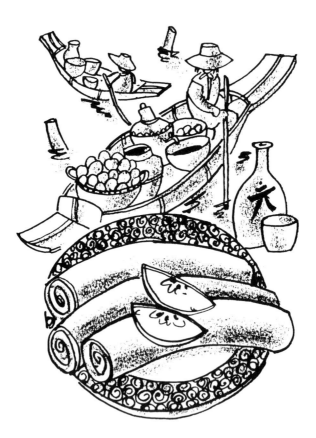

PACIFIQUE (v) (wf)

(Serves 4)

splash of oil

1 onion, finely chopped

1 clove garlic, crushed

2 sticks celery, thinly sliced

1 large green chilli, crushed

1 teaspoon turmeric

juice of 1½ lemons

4 oz (100g) coconut cream

¾ pint (450ml) vegetable stock

1 dessertspoon tomato purée

1 oz (25g) fresh coriander, finely chopped

VEGETABLES:

1 lb (450g) yams, peeled and cut into bite-size pieces

1 yellow plantain, peeled and cut into thick slices

3 oz (75g) okra, tops trimmed

4 oz (100g) babycorn, each one sliced into 3 diagonal pieces

1. Place the oil, onion, garlic, celery, chilli and turmeric in a saucepan and cook until completely soft.

2. Add the lemon juice, stock, coconut cream and tomato purée. Cook until the coconut cream has melted and the sauce has reached the boil. Using a food processor, blend until smooth, season and stir in the finely chopped coriander.

3. Partially cook the yams in boiling salted water. Drain (reserving the water) and add to the sauce so that they finish cooking. (The yams are quite starchy and finishing them off in the sauce helps to thicken it.)

4. Using the same water, cook the babycorn until they are bright in colour and tender. Drain.

5. Cook the okra in the same water until they start releasing their rather slimy juices. Drain and gently rinse.

6. Shallow-fry the plantain (they can be boiled but the flavour is much better when fried). Place in very hot oil, cooking on each side until golden brown. Drain on kitchen paper.

7. As soon as the yams are cooked, stir the vegetables and coriander into the sauce. Adjust the seasoning if necessary and serve with rice.

Cook's tips:
This dish was inspired by a trip to the Caribbean where huge bowls of steaming vegetables in a tangy hot sauce are the norm. Vegetables from the Caribbean are a lot more accessible now, especially from markets. **Yams** need peeling, the skin being brown and quite fibrous. Underneath is a very dense white vegetable, pure carbohydrate and similar to potato.

Plantains, not to be confused with green bananas, are usually bigger in size. The skin must be yellow and starting to blacken in colour so that the plaintain is ripe and sweet inside.

PEA AND CAULIFLOWER SAAR ⓥ ⓦⓕ

(Serves 4)

SAUCE:

splash of oil

1 onion, finely chopped

1 stick celery, finely chopped

20 cardamom pods

2 teaspoons cumin seeds

3 cloves garlic, crushed

1–2 large, green chillis, crushed

2 teaspoons coriander

1 teaspoon paprika

¼ teaspoon nutmeg

8 oz (225g) tomatoes, cut into quarters

2 heaped dessertspoons tomato purée

6 oz (175g) coconut cream

1 oz (25g) fresh coriander, finely chopped

½ pint (300ml) vegetable stock

1 dessertspoon tamari or soy sauce

VEGETABLES:

½ cauliflower, cut into florets

10 oz (275g) frozen peas

10 oz (275g) carrots, cut into thin lengths

9 oz (250g) fresh spinach, any large stalks removed, and washed thoroughly

1. Dry roast the cardamom pods and cumin seeds in a heavy pan (no oil is required) until lightly browned and they are starting to release their aroma. Grind the seeds in a pestle and mortar or in a coffee grinder.

2. Fry all the spices in hot oil with the garlic, chilli, onion and celery. Cook for five minutes until tender.

3. Add the tomatoes to the onion mixture (this should prevent the mixture from sticking). Cook for a further ten minutes.

4. Stir in the tomato purée, stock and coconut cream. Cook gently until the coconut has dissolved. Remove from the heat and, using a food processor, blend until the sauce is thick and smooth.

5. Season the sauce with the coriander, salt, pepper and a splash of tamari.

6. Cook the cauliflower and carrots together in a pan of boiling salted water. Cook until just soft, then drain.

7. Cook the spinach in a saucepan with salt, pepper and a pinch of nutmeg (no water is necessary) until the leaves are limp and the colour is bright green. Drain and squeeze out any excess liquid.

8. Combine the sauce with the vegetables and cook for a further few minutes until the peas are tender. Serve with rice.

Cook's tips:
Roasting chillis greatly improves their flavour, however never burn them as the smell is terrible and will require immediate kitchen evacuation!
This sauce is also excellent as a soup. Just add more stock and omit the vegetables.

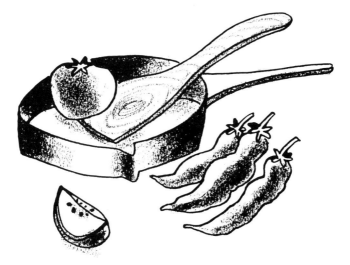

RAJASTHANI BAKE ⓥ ⓦⓕ

(Serves 6)

SAUCE:
olive oil

1 lb 4 oz (575g) red peppers, halved

1 onion, finely chopped

3 teaspoons curry powder

½ large green chilli

1 × 14 oz (400g) tin chopped tomatoes

2 dessertspoons mango chutney

1 oz (25g) fresh coriander, finely chopped

1 teaspoon turmeric

VEGETABLES:
8 oz (225g) mushrooms, sliced

4 oz (100g) French beans, topped, tailed and cut in half

8 oz (225g) carrots, cut into rounds

1 medium-sized cauliflower, cut into florets

1 lb (450g) sweet potatoes, scrubbed and thinly sliced for the topping

1. Preheat the oven to 400°F/200°C/Gas Mark 6.

2. Brush the peppers with olive oil and roast under a hot grill for 5–10 minutes until blistered and slightly blackened. Leave to cool. Pull out the seeds and gently peel away the skin, discarding both.

3. Place the onion, curry powder and chilli in a saucepan with a little olive oil. Cook for 5 minutes until soft. Add the tinned tomatoes, mango chutney and roasted peppers.

4. Using an electric food processor, blend the sauce until smooth, then stir in the coriander. Season to taste.

5. Add the mushrooms to the sauce and cook gently until soft.

6. Cook the French beans and carrots together in boiling salted water until soft. Drain.

7.   Cook the cauliflower with half a teaspoon of turmeric in boiling salted water until just soft. Drain.

8.   Combine all the vegetables with the sauce and place in an ovenproof dish.

9.   Cook the sweet potatoes in boiling salted water for 5 minutes. Drain. Arrange the potatoes over the top of the vegetables so that they are completely covered. Bake in the oven for 15 minutes until lightly brown on top. Serve.

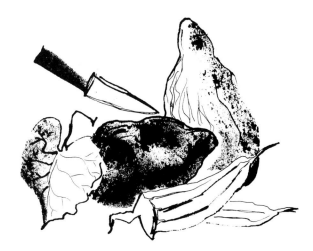

SHEPHERDESS PIE

(Serves 6)

SAUCE:

1 oz (25g) butter

1 onion, finely chopped

fresh thyme and rosemary, pulled off the stalk and chopped

1 small leek, thinly sliced

1 carrot, grated

1 teaspoon paprika

2 heaped dessertspoons wholemeal flour

1 pint (600ml) vegetable stock

1 dessertspoon yeast extract

1 dessertspoon tomato purée

2 dessertspoons soy sauce

1 dessertspoon dry mustard powder

VEGETABLES:

5 oz (150g) dried aduki beans (soaked overnight then simmered for approximately 45 minutes)

1 lb 4 oz (575g) leeks, thinly sliced

12 oz (350g) carrots, sliced into rounds

1½ lb (1.5kg) parsnips, sliced into thick chunks

TOPPING:

3 lb (1.13kg) potatoes, peeled and cut into small chunks

1 oz (25g) butter

¼ pint (150ml) milk

4 oz (100g) vegetarian cheddar, grated

salt and pepper

1. Preheat the oven to 400°F/200°C/Gas Mark 6.

2. Peel the potatoes and place in a saucepan of cold salted water. Cook until soft. Drain.

3. In a saucepan place the butter, onion, leeks, carrots, paprika, thyme and rosemary. Cook until completely soft. Reduce the temperature and stir in the flour. Cook for a few minutes until the texture of the roux changes to that of breadcrumbs.

4. Gradually add the vegetable stock and mustard powder, yeast extract, soy sauce and tomato purée. Using a food processor, blend the sauce until smooth. Bring up to the boil and season.

5. Place the parsnips, sprinkled with oil and salt, on a baking tray and cook until golden brown on top (approximately 15 minutes). Remove from the oven and reduce the heat to 350°F/175°C/Gas Mark 3. Stir-fry the leeks in butter until soft. Cook the carrots in boiling salted water until just soft. Drain.

6. Combine the sauce with the aduki beans and vegetables and turn out into a deep ovenproof dish.

7. Prepare the topping by mashing the potatoes with the butter, milk, salt and pepper until smooth and free of lumps. Stir in the cheese.

8. Top the sauce and vegetables with the mashed potatoes and bake in the oven for 35 minutes until golden brown.

Cook's tips:
Aduki beans are small reddish brown beans that can be found in most health food shops.

This is a very traditional vegetarian dish and, with the addition of yeast extract and soy sauce, it is given a very 'meaty' flavour.

SPANISH CHILLI ⓥ ⓦⓕ

(Serves 4)

SAUCE:

olive oil

1 onion, finely chopped

1 red pepper, cored, de-seeded and chopped into squares

1 clove garlic, crushed

1 large fresh green chilli (or to taste), thinly sliced

4 fresh tomatoes, quartered

1 small carrot, grated

1 × 14 oz (400g) tin plum tomatoes

2 heaped dessertspoons tomato purée

2 oz (50g) ground almonds

3 fl oz (90ml) sherry

1 oz (25g) fresh coriander, chopped

VEGETABLES:

2 oz (50g) red or black dried kidney beans (soaked overnight and simmered for approximately 1 hour)

½ red pepper, cored, de-seeded and sliced into strips

½ green pepper, cored, de-seeded and sliced into strips

1 aubergine, cut into bite-size pieces

2 carrots, sliced into rounds

1 small cauliflower, cut into florets

1. For the sauce: place the oil in a large saucepan with the onion, garlic, chilli, carrot, fresh tomatoes and red pepper. Cook gently for 10 minutes until the mixture is soft.

2. Stir in the tinned tomatoes, tomato purée, ground almonds and sherry. Cook for 5 minutes then, using a food processor, blend the sauce until it is smooth. Stir in the coriander.

3. To prepare the aubergine, cut into chunks and sprinkle with salt. Leave for 15 minutes. Rinse and squeeze any excess liquid from the flesh. Stir-fry the aubergine and peppers together until the aubergine is soft.

4. Cook the cauliflower and carrot together in boiling salted water until tender. Drain.

5. Combine the sauce with the vegetables and kidney beans. Cook the dish for a further few minutes until hot, then serve.

Cook's tips:

An excellent garnish is roasted flaked almonds and slices of avocado.

Ideally this dish should not be eaten on the day that it is made as the flavours are greatly enhanced if left overnight.

A variation on a Spanish Chilli is to omit the sherry and almonds, adding the equivalent quantity of stock instead. Then stir in $1/2$ oz (12g) dark, bitter chocolate. This is a traditional Mexican Chilli. The chocolate adds not only a depth of colour but also a slightly bittersweet taste against the heat of the chilli.

SOUTH INDIAN CAULIFLOWER AVIAL (wf)

(Serves 4)

SAUCE:

splash of oil

2 red onions, finely chopped

2 small green chillis, to taste

1 clove garlic, crushed

1 teaspoon turmeric

3 teaspoons mustard seeds

20 cardamom pods

4 oz (100g) coconut cream

6 fl oz (180ml) stock

5 oz (150g) natural yoghurt

1 oz (25g) fresh coriander, chopped

VEGETABLES:

9 oz (250g) button mushrooms

½ medium-sized cauliflower, cut into florets

4 oz (100g) frozen peas

6 oz (175g) carrots, cut into rounds

1 lb (450g) potatoes, thinly sliced

1 red onion, cut in half and thinly sliced

fresh coriander

1. Preheat the oven to 400°F/200°C/Gas Mark 6.

2. Lightly roast the mustard seeds and cardamom pods in the oven or under a grill until just brown (taking care not to burn them). Grind in a pestle and mortar or coffee grinder.

3. In a saucepan fry the onions, garlic, chilli, turmeric, cardamom and mustard seeds with the oil until soft (approximately 5 minutes).

4. Add the coconut cream and stock. Continue to cook, stirring all the time until the coconut cream has completely dissolved.

5. Remove from the heat and cool for a few minutes. Using an electric food processor, blend the sauce, slowly adding the yoghurt until it is smooth. Season with salt, pepper and fresh coriander. Set aside.

6. Stir-fry the mushrooms then add to the sauce with the frozen peas.

7. Cook the cauliflower and carrots in boiling salted water until the vegetables are just cooked. Drain and combine with the sauce.

8. Place the potatoes and sliced onion in boiling water until the potatoes are soft but not falling apart. Drain.

9. Pour the sauce and vegetables into an ovenproof dish. Layer the mixture of potato and onion on top.

10. Cook in the oven for 25 minutes until lightly brown on top. Garnish with chopped coriander.

Cook's tips:
Make sure that the sauce has cooled before adding the yoghurt so that it does not curdle.

SPINACH ROULADE WITH RICOTTA CHEESE, ASPARAGUS AND DILL ⓦⓕ

(Serves 10)

2½ lbs (1.5kg) frozen spinach, defrosted	2 oz (50g) fresh dill, chopped
10 eggs, separated	4½ oz (125g) fresh asparagus spears
salt and pepper	8 dessertspoons Parmesan cheese
pinch of nutmeg	
14 oz (400g) ricotta cheese	

1. Preheat the oven to 375°F/180°C/Gas Mark 4.

2. Line a 12 × 18 inch baking tray with greaseproof paper. Grease generously with butter and sprinkle with Parmesan cheese.

3. Squeeze as much water as possible from the defrosted spinach. Stir the beaten egg yolks into the spinach with the salt, pepper and nutmeg, mixing thoroughly.

4. Whisk the egg whites until they stand up in stiff peaks and fold them into the spinach mixture.

5. Spoon the soufflé mixture onto the prepared baking tray, easing it into the corners. Bake for 15−20 minutes until the roulade is firm to the touch and slightly golden.

6. Leave for 5 minutes to set then gently turn onto greaseproof paper. Strip the original greaseproof paper off and allow to cool.

7. Finely slice the asparagus and cook in boiling salted water for 3 minutes. Drain.

8. Beat the ricotta cheese until soft. Fold in the asparagus, dill, salt and pepper. Spread the mixture evenly over the roulade, making sure it goes right to the edges. Roll it up from the long edge. Trim the ends off with a sharp serrated knife. Garnish with fresh dill and serve.

Cook's tips:
For this particular recipe, frozen spinach is preferable as it is less time-consuming to prepare and gives a denser texture and colour to the roulade. If you prefer fresh spinach then double the quantity.

TEMPURA VEGETABLES

(Serves 3)

SELECTION OF VEGETABLES:
For example: mushrooms
red onion
broccoli
carrot
cauliflower
pieces of bite-size sweet potato

BATTER:
1 egg
½ teaspoon baking powder
4 oz (100g) white flour
⅓ pint (400ml) cold fizzy water

NORI RELISH:
3 sheets Nori seaweed
1 teaspoon sesame oil
6 dessertspoons rice vinegar
2 dessertspoons honey
2 dessertspoons dry sherry
5 dessertspoons soy sauce

1. For the batter: place the flour and baking powder in a bowl. Make a well in the centre and break the egg into it. Using a hand whisk, beat well, slowly adding the fizzy water.

2. For the vegetables: dip each vegetable into the batter, then immediately fry in very hot oil until golden brown.

3. For the relish: toast the Nori sheets under the grill or in a gas flame for a few seconds until it becomes brittle and turns dark green in colour.

4. Place all the ingredients for the relish together in a bowl and, using a hand blender, purée. The texture of the Nori will remain quite coarse.

5. Dip each of the fried vegetables into the relish before eating.

Cook's tips:
Nori is probably the most popular sea vegetable. It is made into sheets in Japan by pressing the seaweed out by hand after drying. It is available in most health food shops.
   Using fizzy water rather than just tap water in the batter makes it much lighter.

THAI COCONUT CURRY (v) (wf)

This recipe was inspired by Martin Wiffin, the Manager of Food For Thought, after one of his many trips to Thailand.

(Serves 4)

STOCK:

¼ oz (6g) Kaffir lime leaves, fresh or dry (keep 5 leaves back)
1 oz (25g) dehydrated galanga, fresh or dry
3 long stalks fresh lemon grass
4 oz (100g) tamarind block
2 pints (1l.150ml) water

SAUCE:

splash of oil
1 onion, finely chopped
1 clove garlic, sliced
1 oz (25g) root ginger, finely chopped
1 stalk lemon grass (using only the white part)
pinch of cinnamon and nutmeg
2 teaspoons cumin seeds, roasted
2 teaspoons coriander seeds, roasted
1 teaspoon turmeric
½ fresh green chilli
1 teaspoon sweet basil seeds, roasted
1½ pints (900ml) lime stock
4 oz (100g) coconut cream

VEGETABLES:

5 oz (150g) button mushrooms, kept whole
1 red pepper, halved, cored, de-seeded and thinly sliced
1 small cauliflower, cut into florets
1 lb (450g) sweet potato
4½ oz (125g) okra, topped and tailed
1 oz (25g) fresh coriander

1. For the stock: cook together all the ingredients bringing up to the boil for approximately 45 minutes to produce a concentrated stock of approximately ½ pint (300ml). Strain.

2. In another saucepan place a small quantity of oil with the onion. Grind the garlic, root ginger, cinnamon, lemon grass, sweet basil seeds, nutmeg, cumin, coriander, turmeric and chilli together in a pestle and mortar until it forms a paste. Add to the onion and cook for approximately 10 minutes until the mixture is soft. Add a little stock if the spices appear to be sticking to the bottom of the pan.

3. Add all the other ingredients (plus the strained stock). Bring up to the boil before seasoning with salt, pepper and fresh coriander. Keep on a low heat and stir in the 5 ripped lime leaves to ensure the sauce has a real tang to it.

4. For the vegetables: stir the sliced peppers and mushrooms into the sauce and allow them to cook in the sauce so that all the flavours are retained.

5. Place the sweet potato on a baking tray with a little oil and salt. Roast in a hot oven until just soft and lightly brown. This takes approximately 10 minutes, much less than an ordinary potato.

6. Cook the cauliflower with a teaspoon of turmeric in salted boiling water. Drain, reserving the liquid.

7. In the same water, cook the okra until they are just starting to release their juices. Drain.

8. Combine the vegetables with the sauce. Adjust the seasoning if necessary and gently bring up to the boil. Serve on a bed of rice or with noodles.

VEGETARIAN IRISH STEW ⓥ

(Serves 4)

SAUCE:

2 oz (50g) margarine

½ onion, finely chopped

1 stick celery, thinly sliced

1 carrot, grated

2 tomatoes, cut into quarters

2 stalks of rosemary and thyme, pulled off the stalk and finely chopped

1 heaped teaspoon mustard powder

2 dessertspoons wholemeal flour

8 fl oz (240ml) Irish stout

2 dessertspoons tomato purée

1 dessertspoon yeast extract

1 dessertspoon soy sauce

1 pint (600ml) vegetable stock

VEGETABLES:

1 lb (450g) parsnips, topped, tailed and cut into chunks

1 small swede, peeled and cut into cubes

8 oz (225g) small Brussel sprouts, outer leaves removed and a cross cut in the bottom

8 oz (225g) carrots, sliced into rounds

12 oz (350g) baby new potatoes, scrubbed but not peeled

1. In a large saucepan melt the margarine then add the onion, celery, carrot, tomato and herbs. Cook until completely soft (approximately 5 minutes).

2. Turn the heat down and stir in the flour and mustard. Cook for 3–4 minutes until the texture of the roux changes to that of breadcrumbs.

3. Stir in the stout, tomato purée, yeast extract, soy sauce and stock. Using an electric blender, process until smooth. Gently bring the sauce up to the boil until it has thickened.

4. Place the swede and parsnip together on a baking tray with a sprinkling of oil and salt and roast at a high temperature until soft and golden. Drain off any surplus oil.

5. In a pan of salted water cook the potatoes and carrot together until tender. Drain.

6. Cook the Brussel sprouts in boiling water until bright in colour and just soft. Drain.

7. Add the sauce to the vegetables, bring gently to the boil and serve.

WEST INDIAN CURRY (v) (wf)

(Serves 4)

SAUCE:

splash of oil

1 onion, finely chopped

1 oz (25g) root ginger, finely chopped

2 cloves garlic, crushed

3 red chillis, finely chopped

2 teaspoons garam masala

4 teaspoons ground coriander

1 teaspoon ground cumin

1 teaspoon turmeric

2 dessertspoons tomato purée

¼ pint (150ml) orange juice

¼ pint (150ml) pineapple juice

splash of tamari or soy sauce

4 oz (100g) coconut cream

½ pint (300ml) stock

juice of ½ lime

1 oz (25g) fresh coriander, chopped

VEGETABLES:

2 oz (50g) okra, tops trimmed

4 oz (100g) babycorn, halved diagonally

1 lb (450g) sweet potato, cut into bite-size pieces

½ medium-sized cauliflower, cut into florets

1. Fry the onion, ginger and all the spices together in a saucepan (lower the heat and add a couple of tablespoons of stock if the mixture starts to stick). Cook until the onion is soft − approximately 5 minutes.

2. Add all the remaining ingredients, except the fresh coriander, and cook gently for 10 minutes. The coconut cream will naturally thicken the sauce.

3. Roast the sweet potato with a little oil and salt in a preheated oven at 375°F/180°C/Gas Mark 4 until lightly golden brown. Drain off any surplus oil.

4. In some boiling salted water cook the cauliflower and babycorn until just tender. Drain, reserving the liquid.

5.   Lastly place the okra in the boiling water and simmer for approximately 3 minutes. Rinse under cold water to remove the slimy liquid that comes from the vegetable during the cooking process.

6.   Add the sauce to the vegetables and season if necessary. Bring gently to the boil. Serve with rice and a garnish of fresh coriander.

Cook's tips:
Suggested accompaniments for this dish are sultanas and roasted dessicated coconut and/or fried plaintain.
   Coconut cream considerably reduces the heat of a spicy dish so you can be more generous with the quantities of chillis and spices. If too hot, add more coconut cream. **Coconut milk** is also good to use but it does not have such a strong flavour nor does it thicken the sauce so well.

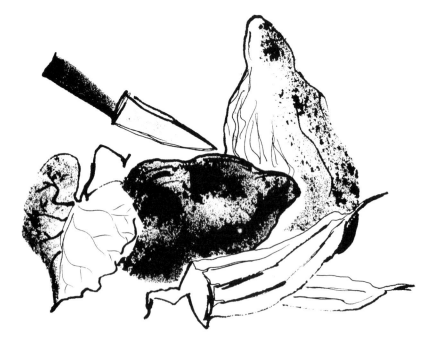

WILD MUSHROOM AND ROCKET RISOTTO

(Serves 4)

1 lb (450g) arborio rice	5 oz (150g) fresh Parmesan cheese (plus 2 oz (50g) for garnish), grated
2 oz (50g) butter	
1 onion, finely chopped	1½ pints (900ml) vegetable stock
3 cloves garlic, crushed	¾ pint (450ml) white wine
8 oz (225g) chanterelle mushrooms, trimmed and halved	
4 oz (100g) rocket, roughly chopped	

1. In a saucepan melt the butter then fry the onion and garlic until soft. Fry the rice with the onion mixture for about 3–4 minutes. This gives the rice a pleasant 'nutty' flavour.

2. Add the stock and wine and cook for approximately 15 minutes, stirring regularly, until all the liquid has been absorbed.

3. Then, over a low heat stir in the mushrooms, rocket, Parmesan, salt and pepper and cook for 3–4 minutes stirring all the time, until the mushrooms are tender.

4. Serve immediately with a garnish of Parmesan cheese.

Cook's tips:
This is a fairly rich dish but the addition of rocket gives it a truly wonderful flavour. **Rocket**, grown in abundance in France and Italy, has become very popular recently and is readily available from supermarkets.

Chanterelle mushrooms smell faintly of apricots. They have a beautiful appearance and are golden yellow in colour. It is a very versatile mushroom for cooking and has a slightly peppery flavour. If chanterelle mushrooms are not available, shitake or oyster mushrooms are equally as good (see page 10).

Arborio rice is a large oval-shaped grain. When the risotto is cooked it must be *al dente* and have the consistency of porridge.

YELLOW SPLIT PEA DAHL (v) (wf)

(Serves 4)

8 oz (225g) yellow split peas
1 red onion, finely chopped
2 cloves garlic, crushed
1 oz (50g) fresh root ginger, finely chopped
½ fresh green chilli, sliced thinly
12 oz (350g) fresh tomatoes, quartered
10 cardamom pods, roasted then ground
2 teaspoons mustard seeds
1 teaspoon ground coriander
1 teaspoon turmeric
1 teaspoon garam masala
2 teaspoons curry powder
1 dessertspoon tomato purée
1 pint (600ml) vegetable stock
juice of ½ lemon
1 oz (25g) fresh coriander, chopped

VEGETABLES:

1 sweet potato, scrubbed and cut into bite-size pieces
6 oz (175g) babycorn, cut in half diagonally
½ green pepper, cored, de-seeded and cut into squares
1 small cauliflower, cored and cut into florets
4 oz mushrooms, sliced
paprika

1. Place the yellow split peas in a large saucepan and completely cover with water. Bring up to the boil then simmer until tender. Drain and rinse well.

2. In the meantime place the onion, garlic, root ginger, chilli, tomatoes and all the spices in a saucepan with oil. Cook until the onion is soft and the tomatoes are a thick pulp.

3. Stir in the lemon juice, tomato purée, stock and half the split peas. Using a food processor, blend until smooth. Season to taste with salt, pepper and coriander.

4. Place the sweet potatoes on a baking tray. Toss with oil, salt and ½ teaspoon of paprika. Roast for approximately 15 minutes until soft.

5. Stir the raw mushrooms into the sauce so that all the juices and flavours released from the mushrooms are contained in the sauce.

6. Cook the cauliflower and babycorn together in boiling salted water with 1 teaspoon of turmeric to make the vegetables a vivid yellow. When tender, drain.

7. Stir the sauce into the remaining split peas and vegetables and gently bring to the boil.

Cook's tips:
The yellow split peas add a wonderful taste and colour. They can, however, be substituted by red or green lentils if desired.

PASTRIES

COOK'S TIPS FOR MAKING GOOD PASTRY

Pastry making should always follow a few basic rules:

1. Everything should be as cold as possible i.e. the butter, your hands, etc.

2. Try not to overwork the pastry. Rub the butter into the flour very lightly but quickly, just using your fingertips.

3. Keep the pastry on the wet rather than the dry side as it makes it a lot easier to handle. You can always add more flour when rolling out.

4. Pastry is basically quite bland and is greatly enhanced by adding flavourings, i.e. alcohol, fresh herbs, seeds (sesame or poppy), cheese or spices.

5. Never turn the pastry over when rolling out and always roll the pastry away from you, not to the sides. This ensures an even distribution of gluten that is present in flour.

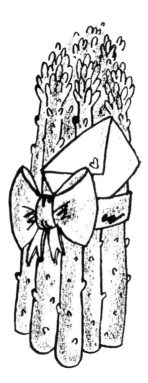

ASPARAGUS AND FETA FILO PARCELS

(Makes 7)

8 oz (225g) asparagus spears, sliced into fairly thick pieces	black pepper
7 oz (200g) feta cheese, diced	1 oz (25g) melted butter
juice of ½ lemon	1 × 10 oz (275g) packet filo pastry, cut in half
½ oz (12g) fresh dill, finely chopped	a few poppy seeds

1. Preheat the oven to 375°F/180°C/Gas Mark 4.

2. Blanch the asparagus in boiling salted water for 2 minutes until it is bright in colour but still crisp. Drain.

3. Place the feta in a bowl and gently combine the asparagus, dill, lemon juice and black pepper.

4. Lay one sheet of filo pastry on a work surface. Brush with melted butter. Place another sheet of filo on top of the first, brush with melted butter and repeat again until there are three layers of filo pastry.

5. Place some of the feta mixture at the nearest end. Fold in the long edges and roll away from you.

6. Brush with butter and sprinkle with a few poppy seeds. Bake in the oven for 15 minutes until golden brown.

Cook's tips:
To prepare asparagus, cut shavings off the end so that it resembles a spear. This removes the tough part. To cook, place upright in boiling salted water with half a lemon and cook for approximately five minutes.

Asparagus are also beautiful eaten raw – just trim off the woody part at the end – excellent as a crudities for dips.

CHEESE AND STOUT RAREBIT PIE

(Serves 4−6)

SAUCE:

1 oz (25g) butter

1 onion, finely chopped

2 cloves garlic, crushed

½ teaspooon nutmeg

1 teaspoon paprika

1 stick celery, thinly sliced

fresh thyme and rosemary, pulled off the stalk and finely chopped

2 dessertspoons white flour

4 fl oz (120ml) stout

1 pint (600ml) milk

7 oz (200g) vegetarian cheddar cheese, grated

VEGETABLES:

2 leeks, sliced on the slant

2 parsnips, cut into long, thick chunks

3 carrots, cut into rounds

1 turnip, peeled and cut into bite-size pieces

PASTRY:

6 oz (175g) white flour

3 oz (75g) butter

½ teaspoon salt

½ teaspoon paprika

1 dessertspoon Parmesan

2 fl oz (60ml) stout

a little milk

1. Preheat the oven to 375°F/180°C/Gas Mark 4.

2. Place the butter in a saucepan with the onion, garlic, celery, nutmeg, paprika, thyme and rosemary. Cook until soft.

3. Reduce the heat and stir in the flour. Cook until the texture of the roux has changed and resembles breadcrumbs.

4. Gradually stir in the stout, milk and cheese, ensuring that no lumps form. Continue cooking until the sauce is thick. Season with salt and pepper.

5. Stir-fry the leeks with a little thyme in a very small quantity of butter. Drain.

6. Put the parsnips on a baking tray sprinkled with oil, salt and rosemary. Bake for approximately 15 minutes until golden in colour. Drain.

7. Put the carrots and turnips together in boiling salted water. Cook until just soft. Drain.

8. Add the vegetables to the sauce and turn out into a pie dish.

9. For the pastry: sieve the flour, salt, Parmesan and paprika into a bowl. Cut the butter into chunks and add to the flour mixture. Using your fingertips, very lightly rub the butter into the flour. Stir in the stout.

10. Turn out onto a floured surface and roll out to fit the top of the pie dish.

11. Using a pastry brush, paint some milk onto the rim of the dish (this prevents the pastry from shrinking and slipping off). Lift the pastry on top of the dish. Trim and finish the edges. Brush the top with a little milk. Make a small incision in the middle of the pastry to allow the steam to escape during cooking. Bake for 30 minutes until golden brown.

Cook's tips:
Only ever use small turnips – they tend to be sweet whereas the larger ones are tough and fibrous.

GOATS CHEESE PURSES
WITH ROASTED RED PEPPER SAUCE

(Makes 6)

14 oz (400g) firm goats cheese, cut into chunks	**2 oz (50g) butter, melted**
1 oz (25g) fresh basil, chopped	**1 × 10 oz (275g) packet filo pastry**
10 marinated sundried tomatoes, cut into thick slices	**SAUCE:**
3 oz (75g) pitted black olives, halved	**2 large red peppers, roasted**
3 dessertspoons Chalice sundried tomato condiment	
1 dessertspoon olive oil	
salt and pepper	

1. Preheat the oven to 400°F/200°C/Gas Mark 6.

2. In a large bowl, mix the goats cheese, basil, sundried tomatoes and paste, olives and olive oil until thoroughly combined. Season to taste. Refrigerate for 15−20 minutes.

3. Lightly brush the pepper halves with oil and place under a hot grill. Allow them to blacken and blister before removing the skin and seeds. Discard.

4. Using a food processor, blend the roasted peppers until they resemble a smooth purée. Place in a saucepan.

5. Place two 8 × 8 inch sheets of filo pastry on top of each other, brushing with the melted butter between each layer. Place one sixth of the filling in the centre. Gather the edges together to form a purse, slightly twist the pastry and press firmly to seal it securely.

6. Brush with butter and place on a greased baking tray. Repeat until all the filling is finished and there are six purses.

7. Bake for 15 minutes until golden brown.

8. Gently warm the pepper sauce and serve immediately with the goats cheese purse and an accompanying mixed leaf salad dressed in balsamic vinegar.

Cook's tips:
During the winter months and early spring the price of red peppers varies dramatically from being ridiculously expensive to fairly reasonable. If they are too expensive, an excellent alternative is to roast 1 lb (450g) whole tomatoes in the oven with a drizzle of olive oil at 375°F/180°C/Gas Mark 4 for 20 minutes until the skin begins to blacken. Then, using a food processor, blend until they resemble a thick purée.

The beauty of roasting both tomatoes and peppers is that they become incredibly sweet, losing any trace of acidity.

HOT HUMMUS PIE ⓥ

(Serves 6)

6 oz (175g) chickpeas (soaked overnight and simmered for 1½ hours – reserve the cooking liquid)	VEGETABLES: 11 oz (300g) broccoli, cut into florets
oil	5 oz (150g) babycorn, cut diagonally in half
2 cloves garlic, crushed	8 oz (225g) mushrooms, cut into slices
1 onion, finely chopped	
3 sticks celery, thinly sliced	1 × 10 oz (275g) packet puff pastry, defrosted
1 large green chilli, crushed	
2 heaped teaspoons ground cumin	
2 heaped teaspoons ground coriander	
juice of 2 lemons	
½ pint (300ml) stock (including the water the chickpeas were cooked in)	
5 dessertspoons light tahini	
1 oz (25g) fresh coriander	

1. Preheat the oven to 375°F/180°C/Gas Mark 4.

2. Fry the onion, celery, garlic, chilli and spices with a little oil. Cook for approximately 10 minutes until completely soft.

3. In a food processor purée the onion mixture with the tahini, chickpeas, stock and lemon juice until smooth. Season with salt and pepper and stir in the finely chopped fresh coriander.

4. Plunge the broccoli into boiling salted water until the colour becomes bright green. Drain, reserving liquid.

5. Cook the babycorn in the same water so that they are still crisp. Drain.

6. Stir-fry the mushrooms with a little oil until they start to release their juices.

7. Mix the vegetables and hummus mixture together (it needs to be of a fairly thick consistency). Place in an ovenproof dish.

8. Roll out the puff pastry and place on top of the vegetable mixture. Make an incision in the middle to allow the steam to escape before baking. Brush with soya milk and sprinkle with a few sesame seeds.

9. Bake for 20 minutes until golden brown.

Cook's tips:
As an alternative filo pastry can be used. This dish is also excellent eaten cold.

MUSHROOM AND ALMOND PATE EN CROUTE WITH CRANBERRY AND ORANGE SAUCE

(Serves 4–5)

1 oz (25g) butter or soya margarine	**CRANBERRY AND ORANGE SAUCE:**
1 onion, finely chopped	8½ oz (227g) fresh cranberries
6 oz (175g) celery, thinly sliced	juice of 1 orange
2 cloves garlic, crushed	4 heaped dessertspoons castor sugar
1 teaspoon paprika	
small quantity fresh thyme and rosemary, pulled off the stalk and chopped	
3 oz (75g) ground almonds	
9 oz (250g) chestnut mushrooms, thinly sliced (see page 56)	
4½ oz (120g) oyster mushrooms, cut into thick slices (see page 10)	
4 oz (100g) shitake mushrooms, cut into thick slices (see page 10)	
2 dessertspoons soy sauce	
9 spring onions, thinly sliced	
2 dessertspoons lemon juice	
12 oz (350g) puff pastry, defrosted	
1 egg, beaten	

1. Preheat the oven to 400°F/200°C/Gas Mark 6.

2. Place the butter in a saucepan with the onion, garlic, celery, paprika and fresh herbs. Cook until just soft.

3. Stir in the mushrooms, soy sauce and lemon juice. Cook until the mushrooms have released their juices.

4. Remove from the heat and stir in the almonds and spring onions so that the pâté is a fairly firm consistency. Season to taste.

5. Roll the pastry out into a large rectangle. Place the mushroom pâté in the middle of the pastry in a long sausage shape (you can pile the pâté up fairly high). With a sharp knife cut out squares of pastry from each corner, cutting almost to the edge of the pâté.

6. Brush the edges with a little of the egg to ensure that the pastry stays together when cooked.

7. Pull the shortest edges over the pâté, then pull the long sides of the pastry over and pinch together forming an attractive ridge along the middle.

8. Brush with egg and bake for 30 minutes until golden brown.

9. For the sauce: place all the ingredients together in a saucepan and cook until soft. Using a food processor, blend the mixture until smooth. Serve hot or cold with the pâté.

Cook's tips:
This is a wonderful festive dish, the mushrooms and cranberries beautifully complimenting each other. Unfortunately the season for fresh cranberries is very short, lasting only between December and January. Make the most of them while you can!

MUSHROOM, SHERRY AND JUNIPER BERRY PIE ⓥ

(Serves 4−5)

SAUCE:

30 dried juniper berries (cooked in a small quantity of water for 20 minutes to soften)

1 oz (25g) soya margarine

1 onion, finely chopped

4 oz (100g) mushrooms, finely chopped

2 sticks celery, thinly sliced

1 sprig of rosemary, pulled off the stalk and finely chopped

2 teaspoons paprika

2 dessertspoons white flour

½ pint (300ml) dry sherry

¾ pint (450ml) vegetable stock

2 dessertspoons soy sauce

1 dessertspoon tomato purée

salt and pepper

VEGETABLES:

2 red onions, cut into approximately 6 chunks

1¼ lb (550g) leeks, finely sliced

1 lb baby new potatoes, scrubbed and kept whole or halved

8 oz (225g) mushrooms, halved

1 medium celeriac (approximately 1 lb (450g) in weight), peeled and cut into bite-size pieces

PASTRY:

4 oz (100g) white flour

2 oz (50g) wholemeal flour

3 oz (75g) soya margarine

½ teaspoon salt

1 teaspoon paprika

10 dessertspoons (approximately) cold water

1. To prepare the sauce: place the margarine, onion, celery, cooked juniper berries, finely chopped mushrooms, rosemary and paprika in a saucepan. Cook for 5−10 minutes until completely soft.

2. Reduce the heat and stir in the white flour to form a roux. Cook for 2−3 minutes until the texture changes to that of breadcrumbs. Slowly add the sherry and vegetable stock, stirring all the time. Add the soy sauce and tomato purée, then using a food processor, blend the sauce until it is completely smooth. Season to taste and return to a low heat for a further 5 minutes to ensure that the flour is completely cooked.

3. To prepare the vegetables: place the potatoes in a pan with cold, salted water. Bring to the boil then simmer until they are soft when a knife is inserted. Drain.

4. Place the red onions on a baking tray with a little olive oil and roast in the oven at 400°F/200°C/Gas Mark 6 for 20 minutes until starting to blacken.

5. Stir-fry the leeks and mushrooms together with a little soya margarine until tender. Drain.

6. Place the celeriac in boiling, salted water and cook until tender. Drain.

7. Stir the vegetables into the sauce and mix well. Adjust seasoning if necessary. Turn out into a pie dish large enough for 4–5 people.

8. For the pastry: place the flour, salt and paprika in a large bowl. Cut the margarine into cubes and add to the flour. Using your fingertips rub the fat into the flour. Stir in the water, gently kneading until the pastry forms a soft ball.

9. Roll the pastry out onto a lightly floured surface until it fits over the top of the sauce and vegetables. Make a small air-hole in the middle and decorate the top with the remaining pieces of pastry.

10. Flute the edges by pinching with your forefinger and thumb. Brush with soya milk. Bake at 375°F/180°C/Gas Mark 4 for 35–40 minutes. Serve immediately.

Cook's tips:
Juniper berries are widely available from supermarkets and health food-shops. The berries should be red-brown to blue-black in colour. They are dried when ripe and used as a condiment but they have a bittersweet flavour and should only every be used sparingly as they can easily dominate a dish.

QUICHE

(Serves 6)

PASTRY:

3 oz (75g) wholemeal flour
3 oz (75g) white flour
½ teaspoon salt
1 teaspoon paprika
1 dessertspoon poppyseeds
3 oz (75g) butter or soya margarine
¼ pint (150ml) cold water
12 oz (350ml) vegetarian cheddar, grated

EGG MIX:

3 eggs
3 fl oz (90ml) sour cream
8 fl oz (240ml) milk

1. Sieve the flours, salt and paprika into a large bowl. Cut the margarine into small chunks and using just your fingertips, rub fat into the flour until it resembles breadcrumbs. Stir in the water and poppyseeds and lightly knead for a couple of seconds.

2. Roll out the pastry so that it fits a 9½ × 10 inch quiche dish.

3. Place a thin layer of cheese on top of the pastry (this prevents it from becoming soggy).

4. Fill the quiche with the vegetables of your choice (see below). Finish the top with the fresh herb or the most attractive vegetable. Season with salt and pepper and layer the remaining cheese over the vegetables so that they are completely covered.

5. Whisk all the ingredients for the egg mix together until light and fluffy. Carefully pour over the vegetables. Beware not to overfill, bearing in mind that the vegetables will release some liquid during the cooking process.

6. Bake at 375°F/180°C/Gas Mark 4 for 15 minutes then reduce the heat to 350°F/160°C/Gas Mark 3 for 30 minutes. Cook until golden brown and firm to the touch. Leave to rest for 10 minutes before serving as this will help it to set.

FILLINGS:

SPINACH:
½ kg (500g) fresh spinach, washed thoroughly

1 oz (25g) fresh dill

½ teaspoon nutmeg

salt and pepper

Cook the spinach with the nutmeg. Drain and squeeze out excess liquid. Mix with the dill.

LEEK AND SAGE:
2 lb (900g) leeks, finely chopped

1 oz (25g) butter

1 oz (25g) fresh sage, pulled off the stalk and chopped

salt and pepper

Stir-fry the leeks and sage with the butter until soft. Drain and season.

CAULIFLOWER, DILL AND GREEN PEPPER:
1 small cauliflower, cut in half, cored and sliced very finely

1 green pepper, cut in half, de-seeded and cut into very thin strips

1 oz (25g) fresh dill, finely chopped

salt and pepper

There is no need to pre-cook the cauliflower. Layer the green pepper and dill on top of the cauliflower. Finish with grated cheese.

BROCCOLI AND CELERIAC:
11 oz (300g) celeriac, peeled and grated

pinch of nutmeg

salt and pepper

8 oz (225g) broccoli, sliced thinly

fresh chervil

Layer the celeriac on top of the broccoli and nutmeg and finish with the grated cheese and chervil.

COURGETTE, RED ONION, SWEETCORN AND TARRAGON:
1 red onion, cut in half and thinly sliced

1 × 12 oz (350g) tin sweetcorn, drained

1 oz (25g) fresh tarragon, pulled off the stalk and chopped

3 courgettes, topped, tailed and thinly sliced

Layer the red onion and sweetcorn on top of the courgettes. Finish with grated cheese and tarragon.

ROASTED RED PEPPER AND RICOTTA PARCELS

(Makes 10)

1½ red peppers, halved	generous bunch chopped basil
1 yellow pepper, halved	1 × 10 oz (275g) packet filo pastry
1 lb (500g) ricotta cheese	oil
1 clove garlic, crushed	sesame seeds

1. Preheat the oven to 400°F/200°C/Gas Mark 6.

2. Lightly oil the peppers and place under a hot grill until the skin starts to blister and blacken. Cool. Discard the seeds and gently pull off the skin. Slice into strips.

3. Beat the ricotta with a spoon until it is smooth. Gently stir in the basil, garlic and peppers.

4. Cut the filo into 6 × 4 inch rectangles. Place two sheets together, generously brushing with oil in between the sheets.

5. Place a spoonful of cheese mixture at the nearest end. Fold in ½ inch of the long side of the filo. This will contain the filling so that it does not escape during cooking.

6. Roll up from the edge nearest you to form a parcel. Lightly brush with oil and sprinkle with a few sesame seeds. Cook for 15−20 minutes until lightly brown.

Cook's tips:
These can be served as they are, hot or cold, as part of a buffet or as a main course accompanied by one of the more substantial salads.

SAMOSAS ⓥ

(Makes approximately 15)

8 oz (225g) frozen peas	1½ heaped teaspoons curry powder
8 oz (225g) carrots, peeled and cubed	1 oz (25g) fresh coriander, finely chopped
1 lb (450g) potatoes, peeled and cubed	1 medium-size packet samosa or spring roll skins
1 clove garlic, crushed	small quantity of white flour
1 fresh green chilli, thinly sliced	oil
2 heaped teaspoons cumin seeds	

1. Stir-fry the carrot and potato with the oil, garlic, chilli, cumin seeds and curry powder.

2. Cook until the potatoes are tender, then stir in the peas. Season with salt, pepper and fresh coriander.

3. Mix a little water with the flour to form a thick paste. Place one skin on a work surface and, using your finger, run a small quantity of paste round the edge. Place another skin on top and repeat with the paste (the flour paste ensures that the skins stay together during frying).

4. Place a spoonful of the potato and carrot mix in the centre of the skin and bring one corner over to the opposite side to form a triangle. Repeat until all the mixture is used up.

5. Deep fry the samosas in *very hot* oil (a wok is ideal for this). Cook until lightly browned and drain on kitchen paper.

Cook's tips:
Samosa skins are available from Chinese supermarkets in three sizes. The very small ones are quite fiddly but are good for buffets. I find using two skins per samosa lessens the risk of them breaking.

As an alternative you can use filo pastry (use 3 layers) for the samosa skins but it makes the samosas slightly more oily and it's also more time-consuming.

SPICED AUBERGINE AND LENTIL FILO PARCELS

(Makes 8 parcels)

2 aubergines kept whole	1 teaspoon ground cumin
1 red pepper, halved	juice of ½ lime
4 oz (100g) green lentils	½ oz (12g) fresh coriander
½ onion, finely chopped	6 oz (175g) feta cheese, cut into cubes
1 clove garlic, crushed	
2 teaspoons curry powder	1 × 10 oz (275g) packet filo pastry
	tabasco (optional)

1. Preheat the oven to 375°F/180°C/Gas Mark 4.

2. With a fork prick the aubergines about six times to allow the steam to escape then brush with oil. Place on a baking tray in the oven and cook for 35 minutes until soft and collapsing in on themselves.

3. Place the lentils in a saucepan and cover with hot water. Cook for approximately 20 minutes until soft. Do not allow to become mushy. Drain and rinse thoroughly until the water runs clear.

4. Brush the pepper with oil and place under a hot grill. Cook until the skin has just started to blacken. When cool, pull out the seeds and gently pull off the skin. Slice into thin strips.

5. In a saucepan fry the onion, garlic, curry powder and cumin with the oil until the mixture is soft. Stir in the lime juice, lentils, strips of pepper and fresh coriander.

6. Cut the aubergine in half and with a spoon gently scoop out the flesh, discarding the skin. Roughly chop the flesh and add to the other ingredients with the cubes of feta cheese. Season the mixture adding a few drops of tabasco if desired (remember feta cheese can be quite salty).

7. Cut the filo pastry into approximately 6 inch squares. Use 2 layers of filo pastry, brushing in between each layer with oil.

8. Place one eighth of the mixture in the middle of the pastry, lift up the sides bringing the pastry to a point above the mixture. Gently twist the pastry so that the edges are all enclosed and it forms an attractive parcel. Brush with oil.

9. Repeat, using up the remainder of the filling. Bake for 20−25 minutes until golden brown. Serve hot or cold.

SPINACH FILO PIE

(Serves 3—4)

½ oz (12g) butter	1 oz (25g) fresh dill
1 medium-sized onion, finely chopped	1 bunch spring onions, thickly sliced
1 clove garlic, crushed	4 oz (100g) feta cheese, cubed
2 sticks celery, finely sliced	4 oz (100g) shitake or oyster mushrooms, sliced (see page 10)
pinch of nutmeg	
1 lb (450g) fresh spinach, any large stalks removed, and thoroughly washed	salt and pepper
	½ of 1 × 10 oz (275g) packet filo pastry
1 heaped dessertspoon Greek yoghurt	a few sesame seeds to garnish
	oil
2 eggs, beaten	

1. Preheat the oven to 375°F/180°C/Gas Mark 4.

2. Place the butter in a saucepan and add the onion, garlic and celery. Cook until soft.

3. Cook the spinach in a separate saucepan with the nutmeg, salt and pepper until just limp. Squeeze out any excess liquid.

4. Using a food processor, blend the onion mixture with the spinach, adding the eggs, dill and yoghurt. Stir in the spring onions and the cubed feta cheese. Season.

5. Stir-fry the mushrooms with a splash of oil and garlic.

6. Spoon the spinach mixture into a pie dish, placing the mushrooms on top. Cover with six layers of filo pastry, brushing liberally with oil between each layer. Score the top of the pastry with a knife and sprinkle with a few sesame seeds. Bake for 10 minutes, then cover with foil to prevent scorching and cook for a further 20 minutes.

7. Serve either hot or cold.

Cook's tips:
When using filo pastry, unlike shortcrust, flaky or puff pastry, there is no need to moisten the edges of the pie dish to prevent the pastry from shrinking, nor do you have to seal the edges. Filo pastry is incredibly easy and versatile to use.

VEGETABLE SPRING ROLLS ⓥ

(Makes 8)

a few drops sesame oil	2 tablespoons Hoi Sin sauce
1 oz (25g) root ginger, finely chopped	1 red pepper, cored, de-seeded then sliced very thinly
3 cloves garlic, crushed	2 oz (50g) frozen peas
4 spring onions, finely chopped	1 packet of large pastry skins (see page 000) or filo pastry
4 oz (100g) beanshoots	
2 carrots, grated	cornflour and water mixed to form a thick paste
4 oz (100g) mushrooms, thinly sliced	oil
½ small tin bamboo shoots, cut into thin strips	salt and pepper

1. In a wok, stir-fry the ginger and garlic in sesame oil for 1–2 minutes before adding all the other vegetables and seasoning. Cook for 2–3 minutes so that the vegetables are still crisp. Remove from the heat.

2. Place two pastry skins together. Using your finger place a small amount of the cornflour paste around the edges. This will prevent the rolls from opening during cooking.

3. Place the vegetable mixture on the long edge nearest to you. Tuck in the edges on each side and roll firmly lengthways.

4. Deep fry in hot oil until golden brown. Drain on kitchen paper and serve.

Cook's tips:
Hoi Sin sauce is a Cantonese speciality used predominantly in Chinese cookery. It is made from a blend of sugar, soya beans, rice vinegar and a little chilli. It is available from most supermarkets as well as Chinese supermarkets.

VEGETABLE STRUDEL WITH LEEK AND PEAR PUREE

(Serves 4)

1 oz (25g) butter	**LEEK AND PEAR PUREE:**
1 onion, finely chopped	1 lb (450g) leeks, trimmed and sliced
1 clove garlic, crushed	1 lb (450g) pears, peeled, cored and sliced
2 large carrots, diced	
8 oz (225g) broccoli, cut into florets	½ pint (300ml) water
8 oz (225g) mushrooms, sliced	2 garlic cloves
1 oz (25g) fresh dill, finely chopped	
pinch of nutmeg	
4 tablespoons plain white flour	
4 tablespoons dry white wine	
5 dessertspoons yoghurt	
2 eggs, lightly beaten	
salt and pepper	
oil	
1 lb (450g) filo pastry	

1. Preheat oven to 375°F/180°C/Gas Mark 4.
2. Fry the onion and garlic with the butter until soft. Add the carrots, broccoli and mushrooms. Cook for approximately 10 minutes until the vegetables are brightly coloured and just tender.
3. Stir in the fresh dill, a pinch of nutmeg, white wine, flour, salt and pepper. Continue cooking for another 5 minutes, stirring regularly. Cool.
4. Beat the egg and yoghurt together. Stir into the cooled vegetable mixture, mixing well.
5. Begin layering sheets of filo pastry in a deep baking tray, brushing lavishly with oil between each sheet.
6. When there are 4 sheets of layered pastry, place the filling in a sausage shape down the middle. Continue layering the pastry on top. Bring the edges together so that the filling is enclosed in pastry. Brush with oil and bake for 35–40 minutes in the preheated oven. The air will seal the edges and prevent them opening during cooking.
7. To make the purée put the leeks, pears and garlic in water and cook for approximately 15 minutes. Drain, blend and season.
8. Serve the vegetable strudel in slices surrounded with the purée.

PASTA

COOK'S TIPS ON COOKING PASTA

1. Pasta should only ever be cooked in rapidly boiling water.

2. Adding garlic to the water is an excellent way of flavouring the pasta.

3. Adding oil stops the pasta from sticking together during the cooking process.

4. Cook pasta so that it is *al dente* and still has a bite to it.

CANNELLONI WITH RICOTTA, PINE KERNEL AND PORCINI FILLING WITH YELLOW TOMATO AND CHEESE SAUCE

(Serves 4–5)

FILLING:

¾–1 lb (350–450g) fresh spinach lasagne

12 oz (350g) fresh spinach, washed thoroughly and any large stalks removed

1½ lb (700g) ricotta cheese

2 oz (50g) pine kernels, ground

2 cloves garlic, crushed

juice of 1 lemon

½ oz (12g) porcini mushrooms (soaked in a little hot water for 10 minutes. Reserve the liquid and thinly slice the mushrooms)

1 oz (25g) fresh basil, finely chopped

YELLOW TOMATO SAUCE:

olive oil

10 oz (275g) yellow tomatoes, cut into quarters

1 small onion, finely chopped

stock from porcini mushrooms

fresh basil, finely chopped

CHEESE SAUCE:

2 oz (50g) butter

2 oz (50g) white flour

¾ pint (450ml) milk

2 heaped dessertspoons Parmesan cheese

1. Preheat oven to 375°F/180°C/Gas Mark 4.

2. Prepare the filling by lightly cooking the spinach in a saucepan until it has just turned limp. Drain, squeezing out any excess liquid and finely chop.

3. Place the ricotta in a large bowl, adding to it the ground pine kernels, crushed garlic, lemon juice, thin strips of hydrated porcini mushrooms, basil and cooked spinach. Mix thoroughly until completely combined. Season to taste then put to one side.

4. Make the yellow tomato sauce by placing the onion and oil in a saucepan. Cook for 2−3 minutes before adding the quarters of tomato. Cook until the mixture resembles a pulp then add the mushroom stock, salt, pepper and fresh basil.

5. Spread the sauce over the bottom of an ovenproof dish.

6. Lay the sheets of lasagne out onto a work surface and cut into squares of approximately 3 inches so that there are 10 squares.

7. Divide the mixture evenly between the 10 squares, making a sausage shape along the top edge with the filling. Gently roll the lasagne around the filling to form a sausage shape and place seam side down on top of the tomato sauce. Repeat until all the mixture has been used up.

8. Make the cheese sauce by melting the butter in a saucepan. Reduce the heat then stir in the flour. Cook the roux for a few minutes until the texture changes to that of breadcrumbs. Add the milk very slowly, stirring all the time to prevent lumps from forming. Stir in the Parmesan cheese and season to taste.

9. Gently pour the cheese sauce over the top of the cannelloni so that they are completely covered (this will prevent the pasta from going crisp on top when cooked).

10. Bake for approximately 40 minutes until golden brown on top. Serve immediately, taking great care when serving not to break the individual cannelloni.

Cook's tips:
This dish could be made using dry cannelloni shells (they do not need pre-cooking but do absorb a lot of sauce so an extra half quantity of cheese sauce would be required). However, it really is just as easy to roll the lasagne yourself and the difference in flavour and the quality of the dish when using fresh pasta is tremendous.

Yellow tomatoes are really only available in the summer, so if they are not around substitute them for plum or regular tomatoes.

GNOCCHI WITH CREAM, PAPRIKA AND FRESH DILL

(Serves 4)

1 medium onion, finely chopped	3 fl oz (90ml) double cream
1 clove garlic, crushed	1 oz (25g) fresh dill, chopped
2 oz (50g) soya margarine or butter	4 oz (100g) oyster mushrooms, cut into strips
2 dessertspoons white flour	1 lb 2 oz (500g) spinach gnocchi
2 heaped teaspoons paprika	juice of ½ lemon
½ pint (300ml) dry white wine	Parmesan cheese
3 fl oz (90ml) milk	

1. Melt the margarine or butter in a saucepan and fry the onion, garlic and paprika until soft. Lower the heat and stir in the flour to form a roux. Cook gently for a few minutes until the consistency changes to that of breadcrumbs.

2. Slowly add the wine, milk and cream, stirring all the time ensuring that no lumps form.

3. Stir in the mushrooms and fresh dill and let them gently cook in the sauce. Season with salt and pepper.

4. Cook the gnocchi in boiling salted water with the juice of half a lemon. The gnocchi is cooked when it floats to the surface. Drain.

5. Add the sauce to the gnocchi. The gnocchi will thicken the sauce when heated together. Serve with freshly ground black pepper and Parmesan cheese.

Cook's tips:
Gnocchi (small balls of potato or spinach) can be bought pre-packed from large supermarkets or Italian delicatessens.

PENNE WITH POTATOES AND PESTO

(Serves 2)

6 oz (175g) penne pasta	small bunch fresh basil, finely chopped
6 oz (175g) cooked potatoes, peeled and sliced	Parmesan to serve
5 heaped teaspoons of Chalice pesto	black pepper

1. Add the pasta to boiling salted water with a splash of oil in it. Cook for 5–10 minutes until *al dente*. Drain reserving two dessertspoons of the water.

2. Put the potatoes, pesto, pasta, reserved pasta water and freshly ground black pepper in a saucepan. Heat, stirring all the time until the potatoes are warm.

3. Serve immediately with a sprinkling of Parmesan cheese and freshly chopped fresh basil.

Cook's tips:
This may sound an unlikely combination but it is a traditional and very tasty Italian dish. The potatoes should be quartered and then cooked. When cool gently pull off the skins and thickly slice. Leftover potatoes are great to use up in this recipe.

RAVIOLI FILLED WITH HAZELNUT AND SUNDRIED TOMATOES

This recipe was devised and tested by Jill Moss,
a chef at Food For Thought.

(Serves 4)

FILLING:

2 oz (50g) ground hazelnuts

4–6 marinated sundried tomatoes, cut into thin strips (see page 51)

1–2 cloves garlic, crushed

1 oz (25g) fresh basil, finely chopped

black pepper

olive oil

PASTA DOUGH:

7 oz (200g) durum wheat flour or unbleached white flour

2 large eggs

salt

1. In a large bowl mix the salt and flour. Make a well in the centre and break the eggs into it. Gently mix, bringing the flour into the well using your fingertips.

2. Turn out onto a lightly floured work surface. Knead well, cover and leave to rest in the fridge for 20 minutes.

3. Prepare the filling by mixing the hazelnuts, garlic, sundried tomatoes, basil and black pepper together. Add enough olive oil to form a moist paste.

4. Make the ravioli by splitting the dough in half. Heavily flour the work surface then roll out one half, stretching the dough as you go (you can turn the dough over). Roll out as thinly as possible.

5. Dot small quantities of the filling evenly onto the sheet of pasta, leaving a good space in between each pile. Moisten around each pile of filling with a little beaten egg or water.

6. Roll out the second half of the dough to the same size and thickness. Place on top of the pasta and filling. Gently press each parcel of ravioli together to seal them. Cut generously around each square with a sharp knife.

7. Gently place in boiling salted and oiled water for approximately 5 minutes or until *al dente*.

8. Serve immediately with your favourite sauce or 4 dessertspoons of Chalice sundried tomato paste.

Cook's tips:
The advantage of this recipe is that no specialist pasta-making equipment is necessary and it is all done very simply by hand. The filling suggested for the ravioli is also wonderful as a pesto sauce to serve with pasta. In this case use crushed hazelnuts rather than ground ones.

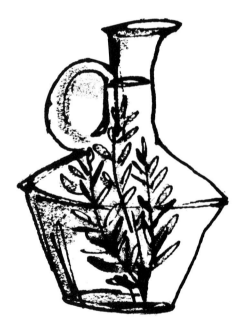

SPINACH, RICOTTA AND PLUM TOMATO LASAGNE

(Serves 4)

TOMATO AND RED WINE SAUCE:

splash of olive oil

½ onion, finely chopped

1 clove garlic, crushed

6 plum tomatoes, skinned

6 fl oz (180ml) tomato juice

4 fl oz (120ml) red wine

2 dessertspoons tomato purée

½ oz (12g) fresh basil, chopped

FILLING:

½ lb (225g) fresh spinach, large stalks removed, and washed thoroughly

4 oz (100g) ricotta cheese

2 heaped teaspoons Chalice pesto

1 clove garlic, crushed

6 oz (175g) button mushrooms

½ medium-sized onion, cut in half moons

2 red peppers, halved, de-seeded, and cut into thin strips

½ lb (225g) fresh spinach lasagne sheets

WHITE SAUCE:

2 oz (50g) margarine or butter

3 dessertspoons white flour

1 pint (600ml) milk

pinch of nutmeg

2 oz (50g) Parmesan

1. Preheat the oven to 400°F/200°C/Gas Mark 6.

2. For the tomato sauce: heat the oil and fry the onion and garlic together until soft. Add the tomatoes and cook until they form a soft pulp.

3. Stir in the tomato purée, red wine and tomato juice and continue to cook for a further 4–5 minutes. Season with salt, pepper and chopped fresh basil.

4. For the filling: slice the raw spinach very thinly and combine with the ricotta and pesto. Set aside.

5. Stir-fry the onions, peppers and garlic together until soft. Set aside.

6. Stir-fry the mushrooms. Set aside.

7. For the white sauce melt the margarine or butter, then stir in the flour. Gently cook for a few minutes. Slowly add the milk, stirring all the time to avoid lumps from forming. Season with salt, pepper and 1 oz (25g) of Parmesan cheese.

8. To assemble: place one third of the tomato sauce in the bottom of a medium-sized ovenproof dish. Cover with a layer of lasagne.

9. Pour over another third of the tomato sauce plus three-quarters of the pepper and onion mixture. Cover with a layer of lasagne.

10. Pour over the spinach mixture. Cover with a layer of lasagne.

11. Pour over the remainder of the tomato sauce, then the remainder of the peppers and the mushrooms. Cover with a layer of lasagne.

12. Finish with the white sauce.

13. Bake for 30 minutes until golden brown. Serve with a sprinkling of the remaining Parmesan cheese.

Pods of nutmeg drying on racks before being graded for use.

TAGLIATELLE WITH LEEKS, CREAM AND PINE KERNELS

(Serves 2−3)

½ oz (12g) butter

1 lb (450g) leeks, trimmed then finely sliced on the diagonal

1 clove garlic, crushed

½ pint (300ml) single cream

1½ oz (35g) pine kernels, stir-fried in olive oil until golden brown

1 heaped dessertspoon Chalice arrabbiata or sundried tomato condiment

9 oz (250g) fresh garlic and herb tagliatelle

grated fresh Parmesan cheese and finely chopped basil to garnish

1. In a large saucepan melt the butter then stir-fry the garlic and leeks until soft.

2. Reduce the heat and stir in the condiment, cream and stir-fried pine kernels. Season to taste.

3. In another saucepan bring some salted water to the boil. Add the pasta, cooking for 5 minutes until *al dente*. Drain.

4. Stir the pasta into the sauce. Serve immediately with a garnish of grated Parmesan, chopped basil and freshly ground pepper.

Cook's tips:
I find that the **half fat cream** that is now available is much better for this recipe as it is less rich and definitely less fattening. **Fromage frais** is also a lighter and healthier alternative.

Supermarkets have responded to people's insatiable appetite for pasta by selling a huge range of fresh pastas of excellent quality. It is well worth experimenting with the different varieties.

TORTELLINI WITH WILD MUSHROOMS AND MASCARPONE CHEESE

(Serves 2−3)

9 oz (250g) spinach and ricotta or mushroom tortellini	1 teaspoon paprika
olive oil	1 dessertspoon soy sauce
6 oz (175g) oyster mushrooms, cut in half (see page 10)	4 fl oz (120ml) brandy
4 oz (100g) field mushrooms, thinly sliced (see page 88)	4 oz (100g) mascarpone or cream cheese
½ oz (12g) dried porcini mushrooms	1 oz (50g) fresh basil to garnish
fresh rosemary, pulled off the stalk and finely chopped	Parmesan cheese
2 cloves garlic	black pepper

1. Bring some salted water, with a splash of oil and a clove of garlic to the boil.

2. In another saucepan place the oil, 1 clove crushed garlic, rosemary, paprika, porcini mushrooms and field mushrooms and cook gently until the mushrooms release their juices.

3. Add the soy sauce, brandy and oyster mushrooms. Continue to cook until the mushrooms are soft and there is a pool of concentrated mushroom juice in the base of the pan. Season. Remove from the heat and stir in the mascarpone until well combined.

4. Tip the tortellini into the rapidly boiling water. Cook until the pasta floats up to the surface (approximately 5−10 minutes).

5. Drain and toss with the mushroom sauce. Serve immediately with black pepper, Parmesan cheese and fresh basil.

Cook's tips:
The dried mushrooms in this recipe do not need to be pre-soaked as they hydrate in the juices from the other mushrooms and in the heat generated during cooking. **Porcini** are expensive but they have a beautiful, strong flavour so very few are needed.

STIR-FRIES

COOK'S TIPS ON ENSURING A GOOD STIR-FRY

The best stir-fries are obtained when using a wok. Before you start cooking, ensure that both the wok and the oil are hot. The idea is to 'flash' cook the vegetables so that the flavours are quickly sealed in. This ensures the colour, texture and nutritional content are all retained. The whole cooking process should take a maximum of 10 minutes.

Most vegetables can be stir-fried but it is worth taking time in their preparation ensuring they they are finely and attractively cut, preferably so that the completed dish comprises of various shapes and colours of vegetables.

The sauces need to be very concentrated as they quickly lose their intensity when added to the vegetables. The combination of adding nuts, fruit, seaweed, tofu and by serving on a bed of rice or noodles proves to be a highly nutritious, quick, well-balanced and delicious meal.

CHINESE STIR-FRY (v)(wf)

(Serves 3)

VEGETABLES:
8 oz (225g) courgettes, cut in half lengthways and then cut on the slant

9 oz (250g) mushrooms, thinly sliced

8 oz (225g) carrots, cut into matchsticks

9 oz (250g) broccoli, cut into small florets

1 bunch spring onions, using the green, cut into three then slice each section in very thin lengths

7 oz (200g) beansprouts

8 oz (225g) tin of water chestnuts, sliced

CHINESE SAUCE:
splash of oil

2 cloves garlic

2 tablespoons tamari or soy sauce

2 heaped teaspoons ground ginger

1. Make the sauce by putting the garlic and ginger together in a pestle and mortar and grind until they form a paste. Add the tamari.

2. Place the oil in a wok and heat. Cook the vegetables in the following order: carrots, mushrooms and broccoli, courgettes, water chestnuts, salt to taste and sauce, beanshoots and spring onions.

3. Serve immediately with rice or noodles.

JAPANESE STIR-FRY WITH TERYAKI SAUCE

(Serves 4)

¼–½ oz (6–12g) arame seaweed (no need to pre-soak)

1 orange pepper, halved, de-seeded and cut into thin slices

8 spring onions, cut into diagonal thick slices

6 oz (170g) babycorn, cut diagonally in half

5 oz (150g) mangetout, topped, tailed and cut diagonally in half

3 sticks celery, cut into matchsticks

9 oz (250g) mushrooms, thinly sliced

2 carrots, cut into matchsticks

4 oz (100g) tofu, cut into small cubes

sesame oil to cook

TERYAKI SAUCE:
2 cloves garlic

2 teaspoons ground ginger

2 dessertspoons plum sauce

2 dessertspoons rice vinegar

2 dessertspoons honey

3 dessertspoons tamari or soy sauce

1 teaspoon dry mustard

salt

1. Make the sauce by crushing the garlic and ginger together in a pestle and mortar then combine all the sauce ingredients together.

2. Cook the vegetables with the sesame oil in the following order: carrots and celery, babycorn and arame, peppers, mushrooms, tofu, salt and sauce, mangetout and spring onions.

3. Serve immediately while the vegetables are still fresh and crisp on a bed of rice or noodles.

BREADS

COOK'S TIPS FOR BREADMAKING

MAKING YEAST GROW:

Yeast comes to life from a dormant state when it first comes into contact with moisture (i.e. the tepid water). Sugar is required to enable the yeast to grow and, as it grows, it gives off waste products, one of which is carbon dioxide, a gas which accumulates in the dough, causing it to rise and expand. This process requires warmth.

Using fresh yeast or dry: When using fresh yeast, crumble it into a small bowl. Add the sugar and enough warm water to generously cover it. Leave for approximately 10 minutes or until frothy. Dried yeast can be added directly to the other dry ingredients. It will activate during the first proving.

What is gluten?: Gluten is a group of proteins found in the wheat kernel. It can be found in wholemeal and white flours and is present after the wheat is ground into the flour.

Where is the best place for dough to rise?: The best temperature to 'prove' dough is human body temperature. Using either a gas or an electric oven, turn the stove to 'warm' for 10 minutes, turn it off and leave the dough there to rise. Always cover with a damp teatowel or cling-film so that the dough does not dry out on top.

Is it possible to over- or under-knead bread?: If kneading by hand it is impossible to over-knead but if using a mixer with a dough attachment it is easy to overdo it. This causes over-developed gluten and therefore a toughened loaf. With a dough hook, use a low speed and watch it carefully. Dough has been kneaded sufficiently when it acquires the consistency of an ear lobe. If you under-knead the loaf it will closely resemble a brick! Average kneading time by hand is 15−20 minutes of vigorous activity.

HOW TO CHOOSE THE RIGHT FLOUR:

Wholewheat 'bread' flour has a higher percentage of gluten than other wholewheat flours. It is sometimes called 'high protein' flour. The gluten content relates to the type of wheat involved.

Wholewheat pastry flour is more finely milled and lower in gluten than 'bread' flour. The lower gluten makes it a better choice for flaky pastry, eg. pie crusts, biscuits, pancakes, cakes or, in short, most baked goods apart from bread.

Bleached and unbleached white flour: the major complaint against bleached white flour is that it contains residues from its chemical bleaching agents, however unbleached is less refined and has a much fresher taste.

SUNDRIED TOMATO BREAD (v)

12 marinated sundried tomatoes, no need to slice (see page 00)	3 dessertpoons Chalice sundried tomato condiment

Substitute the oil for the equivalent quantity of oil that the tomatoes were marinated in.

ALMOND SCONES (v)

(Makes 10)

1 lb (450g) plain white flour	*2 oz (50g) whole almonds, finely chopped or flaked
3 level teaspoons baking powder	½ pint (300ml) unsweetened soya milk
6 oz (75g) soya margarine	
2 oz (50g) brown sugar	
*2 teaspoons natural almond essence	

1. In a large bowl sieve the flour and baking powder together. Using your fingertips rub the fat into the flour until it resembles breadcrumbs.

2. Stir in the sugar, almond essence and chopped almonds. Mix in the soya milk so that the dough is soft and moist.

3. Turn the dough out onto a lightly floured work surface and gently knead. Using the palm of your hand flatten the mixture until 1½ inches deep. Using a 2 inch scone cutter, cut out approximately 10 scones and place onto an oiled and floured baking tray. Lightly brush each one with soya milk.

4. Bake at 400°F/200°C/Gas Mark 6 for approximately 20 minutes or until golden brown on top. Cool on a wire rack or serve hot with jam, cream or yoghurt.

VARIATIONS

COCONUT AND LEMON SCONES (v)

Omit the * ingredients and substitute 2 oz (50g) dessicated coconut and the zest and juice of 1 lemon.

CHOCOLATE AND SULTANA SCONES (v)

Omit the * ingredients and substitute 4 oz (100g) sultanas and 4 dessertspoons of cocoa powder.

STRAWBERRY SCONES (v)

Omit the * ingredients and substitute 4 heaped dessertspoons of unsweetened strawberry jam plus 4 oz (100g) of thinly sliced strawberries (reduce the quantity of soya milk to 8 fl oz/240ml). Use the same quantities for raspberry and blackberry scones.

Cook's tips:
Food For Thought vegan scones are a firm favourite at any time of the day but particularly for breakfast, hot from the oven. In the summer we make them using a variety of berries and complimentary sugar-free jams. They are also very good if brushed with a little apple concentrate straight from the oven as this makes them slightly sticky, sweet and glossy on top.

CAKES

PEANUT FLAPJACKS

8 oz (225g) soya margarine	3 oz (75g) peanuts
2 oz (50g) demerara sugar	6 oz (175g) large oats
2 oz (50g) honey	6 oz (175g) small oats
2 oz (50g) peanut butter	

1. Preheat the oven to 300°F/150°C/Gas Mark 2.

2. In a saucepan melt the margarine, sugar, honey, peanuts and peanut butter. Cook until the sugar has completely dissolved and the mixture is boiling.

3. Remove from the heat and thoroughly stir in the oats. The mixture should be quite firm.

4. Turn the mixture onto a well-greased tray (approximately 10 × 6½ inches, 1½ inches deep). Press the mixture down firmly, using the back of a wooden spoon.

5. Bake for between 20−30 minutes or until lightly browned. Leave the flapjacks for 15 minutes before cutting into the required size and preferably leave until the next day before eating.

VARIATIONS

Add the ingredients for each variation to the sugar, margarine and honey mixture in the original recipe and omit the peanuts and peanut butter.

APPLE AND WALNUT FLAPJACKS

2 medium cooking apples, cored and grated	2 oz (50g) walnuts

COCONUT FLAPJACKS

3 oz (75g) coconut cream	2 oz (50g) dessicated coconut

SESAME AND TAHINI FLAPJACKS

2 dessertspoons light tahini   2 oz (50g) sesame seeds

Cook's tips:
Take care when removing the flapjacks from the tin that they do not break and crumble. It is best to cook them then cut them immediately. Leave overnight to get hard then recut them and ease them from the tin.
   If stored in an airtight container they will keep well for up to 4 days.

BANANA CAKE

8 oz (225g) butter or soya margarine	1 teaspoon baking powder
8 oz (225g) brown sugar	2 large bananas or 3 medium bananas, mashed
1 teaspoon vanilla essence	3 eggs, beaten
3 oz (75g) sultanas	
4 oz (100g) white flour, sieved	
4 oz (100g) wholewheat flour, sieved	

1. With an electric mixer cream the butter and sugar together until pale and fluffy. Continue beating the mixture whilst slowly adding the beaten eggs and vanilla essence. Beat in the bananas.

2. Using a metal spoon, fold in the white and brown flour plus the baking powder and sultanas.

3. Turn the mixture into a greased and lined 2 lb loaf tin. Bake for 30 minutes at 375°F/180°C/Gas Mark 4 then for a further 30 minutes at 300°F/150°C/Gas Mark 2 until golden brown and an inserted skewer comes cleanly out of the centre.

Cook's tips:
This cake will keep well for several days. It is also good served with butter as its texture is similar to bread.

When folding flour into a cake mixture it is always advisable to use a metal spoon. The flour is the heaviest ingredient and must be gently incorporated into the beaten butter, sugar and eggs which are light and fluffy. A metal spoon will give a lighter touch and is preferable to a wooden one which will knock some of the air out of the mixture.

CARROT CAKE

8 fl oz (240ml) sunflower oil	TOPPING:
8 oz (225g) brown sugar	6 oz (175g) cream cheese
2 fl oz (60ml) orange juice	2 oz (50g) butter
3 eggs, lightly beaten	6 oz (175g) icing sugar, sieved
½ teaspoon vanilla essence	1 teaspoon vanilla or orange essence
¼ teaspoon nutmeg	
½ teaspoon ground cinnamon	zest or segments of orange to decorate
1 heaped teaspoon baking powder	
10 oz (275g) wholemeal flour, sieved	
10 oz (275g) grated carrot	
3 oz (75g) raisins	

1. Preheat the oven to 300°F/150°C/Gas Mark 2.

2. Whisk the oil, sugar and orange juice together then slowly drizzle in the eggs in approximately five stages, beating well between each addition.

3. Fold the flour, baking powder, vanilla essence and spices into the sugar and orange juice mixture. When it is of a smooth consistency fold in the carrots and raisins.

4. Pour into a greased and lined 2 lb loaf tin and bake in the preheated oven for 1¼ hours, or until a skewer inserted into the middle of the cake comes out cleanly.

5. Leave to stand in the tin for 15 minutes before turning out onto a wire rack.

6. For the topping: cream the butter and cheese together, then stir in the icing sugar and essence until it is a smooth consistency. Spread over the top of the cake. Decorate with segments of orange or orange zest.

Cook's tips:
This cake is also delicious served hot (without the topping) with yoghurt or ice cream.

CHEESE CAKE

8 oz (225g) soft margarine	8 oz (225g) white flour, sieved
8 oz (225g) castor sugar	1 teaspoon baking powder
½ teaspoon vanilla essence	2 oz (50g) sultanas
4 eggs, lightly beaten	juice and zest of 1 lemon
6 oz (175g) light cream cheese	

1. Preheat the oven to 375°F/180°C/Gas Mark 4.

2. Place the margarine and sugar in a bowl and using an electric whisk, beat until light and fluffy.

3. Still using the whisk add the vanilla essence. Drizzle in the eggs then add the cream cheese.

4. Using a metal spoon fold in the flour, baking powder, sultanas, lemon juice and zest.

5. Turn the mixture into a greased and lined 7 inch cake tin and bake in the middle of the preheated oven for 1 hour, or until firm to the touch and golden brown.

6. Leave to stand for 10 minutes then turn out onto a wire rack to cool.

Cook's tips:
A good topping for this cake is the same as the one used for carrot cake, replacing the vanilla or orange essence with lemon essence.

CHOCOLATE CAKE

8 oz (225g) soft margarine	1 heaped dessertspoon golden syrup
8 oz (225g) castor sugar	
½ teaspoon vanilla essence	3 dessertspoons milk
3 eggs, lightly beaten	2 oz (50g) plain chocolate, grated
2 oz (50g) cocoa powder, sieved	white and milk chocolate shavings for garnish
6 oz (175g) plain white flour, sieved	
1 teaspoon baking powder, sieved	

1. Preheat the oven to 375°F/180°C/Gas Mark 4.

2. In a bowl, cream the margarine and sugar together with an electric whisk until light and fluffy.

3. Still using the electric whisk add the essence, then slowly add the eggs.

4. Using a metal spoon, fold in the remaining ingredients until it is a smooth and lump-free consistency.

5. Turn the mixture into a greased and lined 7 inch cake tin and bake in the middle of the oven for 1–1¼ hours or until a skewer inserted in the middle of the cake comes out cleanly.

6. Leave the cake for 10 minutes to cool then turn out onto a wire rack.

7. When the cake is completely cool, garnish it with shavings of white and milk chocolate (use a potato peeler) and a dredging of icing sugar.

Cook's tips:
To make a good chocolate sauce, melt some plain chocolate with a little cream in a bowl that is sitting in a saucepan of boiling water. Stir until smooth, then spread over the top of the cake with a palette-knife.

Beware not to overcook chocolate cake as it will make it very dry. I always think the best chocolate cakes are moist and gooey.

COCONUT AND LIME CAKE

8 oz (225g) margarine	**TOPPING:**
8 oz (225g) castor sugar	juice and zest of 2 limes
4 oz (100g) coconut cream (placed in a bowl and covered with boiling water until it melts)	6 oz (175g) icing sugar, sieved
3 eggs	
8 oz (225g) plain white flour, sieved	
1 teaspoon baking powder	
juice and zest of 2 limes	

1. Preheat the oven to 300°F/150°C/Gas Mark 2.

2. In a large bowl cream the margarine and sugar together using an electric whisk until light and fluffy.

3. Add the lime zest and the eggs, one at a time, whisking well between each addition.

4. Using a metal spoon fold in the sieved flour and baking powder then the lime juice and melted coconut cream.

5. Turn the mixture into a greased and lined 7 inch cake tin. Bake in the middle of the preheated oven until firm to the touch and lightly golden in colour.

6. After 10 minutes turn the cake onto a wire rack. Leave to cool.

7. To make the topping: mix the sieved icing sugar into the lime juice until it is a thick consistency. If it is too thin it will not stay on top of the cake.

8. When the cake is completely cold spread the icing evenly over the top. Decorate with long thin strips of lime peel.

LEMON AND POPPYSEED CAKE

8 oz (225g) soft margarine	8 oz (225g) white flour, sieved
8 oz (225g) castor sugar	1 teaspoon baking powder
3 eggs, lightly beaten	2 dessertspoons poppyseeds
zest and segments of 2 lemons	

1. Preheat the oven to 375°F/180°C/Gas Mark 4.

2. In a bowl place the margarine and sugar together. Using an electric whisk cream the two together until light and fluffy.

3. Slowly add the eggs, beating well.

4. With a metal spoon fold in the lemon zest and segments, flour, baking powder and poppyseeds.

5. Turn the mixture into a 7 inch greased and lined cake tin. Bake in the middle of the oven for 1 hour until golden and firm.

6. Leave the cake to stand for 10 minutes before turning out onto a wire rack to cool completely.

Cook's tips:
This is one of my favourite cakes – the texture of the poppyseeds and zip from the lemon are delicious.

The maximum flavour comes from the lemon segments. The best way to separate the segments from the pith is to cut away the skin using a sharp knife. Then slice as close to the pith as possible, releasing the segment of the lemon.

MARMALADE CAKE

1 lb (450g) white flour, sieved	zest of 2 oranges
1½ level teaspoons baking powder	6 fl oz (180ml) orange juice
	3 eggs, lightly beaten
6 oz (175g) castor sugar	
½ teaspoon salt	TOPPING:
½ teaspoon nutmeg	4 oz (100g) marmalade
8 oz (225g) butter	
10 oz (275g) coarse orange marmalade	

1. Preheat the oven to 350°F/160°C/Gas Mark 3.

2. Sieve the dry ingredients into a bowl.

3. In a small saucepan heat the butter, marmalade, orange zest and orange juice until the butter has melted. Leave to cool.

4. Stir into the dry ingredients with the beaten egg.

5. Pour into a greased and lined 7 inch cake tin. Bake in the preheated oven for 1½ hours, or until a skewer inserted into the middle of the cake comes out cleanly. Cool in the tin for 20 minutes then turn out onto a wire rack.

6. To make the topping: place the marmalade in a saucepan and gently heat until it has melted. Spread over the top of the cake.

RUM AND CHOCOLATE CAKE

2 oz (50g) plain chocolate	5 dessertspoons rum essence
4 oz (100g) soya margarine	¼ pint (150ml) milk
10 oz (275g) brown sugar	2 dessertspoons lemon juice
2 eggs, separated	½ teaspoon vanilla essence
4 oz (100g) raisins	grated chocolate and icing sugar to decorate
10 oz (275g) white flour, sieved	
1 teaspoon baking powder	

1. Preheat the oven to 375°F/180°C/Gas Mark 4.

2. Melt the chocolate in a small bowl set in a pan of water over a low heat.

3. Cream the margarine and sugar together with an electric whisk until light and fluffy. Beat in the egg yolks and melted chocolate.

4. Using a metal spoon, fold in the flour, baking powder and raisins then add the rum, lemon juice, vanilla essence and milk until it is a smooth consistency.

5. In a separate bowl whisk the egg whites until stiff then fold into the cake mixture.

6. Pour into a greased and lined 7 inch cake tin and bake in the preheated oven for 1¼–1½ hours, or until a skewer inserted in the middle of the cake comes out cleanly.

7. Leave the cake to stand for 15 minutes before turning out onto a wire rack.

8. When completely cool decorate with a dredging of icing sugar and grated chocolate.

Cook's tips:
The best **rum essence** is homemade. Place a large quantity of cloves, cinnamon, a whole nutmeg, bay leaves and mace in a jar and cover with dark rum. Leave this for a minimum of two weeks then drain the rum off and use in cakes, desserts and drinks. Keep the spices and cover again with rum (this can be done four times).

DESSERTS

ALMOND PANCAKES FILLED WITH RICOTTA, BLACK CHERRY AND CASSIS

(Makes four 11 inch pancakes or eight 6 inch pancakes)

BATTER:	FILLING:
4 oz (100g) white flour	10 oz (275g) ricotta cheese
pinch of salt	2 dessertspoons honey
2 eggs, beaten	1 dessertspoon crème de cassis
8–10 fl oz (240–300ml) milk	1 × 15 oz (425g) tin pitted black cherries, drained (use fresh if in season)
2 dessertspoons oil	
1 oz (25g) flaked almonds	icing sugar, sieved for garnish

1. Place the flour and salt in a large mixing bowl and make a well in the centre. Add the eggs then slowly whisk in the milk and oil ensuring that no lumps form. Stir in the almonds and leave to 'rest' in the fridge.

2. Prepare the filling by placing the ricotta, honey and crème de cassis in a food processor. Blend until completely smooth then stir in the whole black cherries.

3. Cook the pancakes (see page 95).

4. While the pancakes are still warm, spread the ricotta mixture over half of the pancake, fold the other half over the mixture then fold in half again.

5. Serve immediately with a sprinkling of sieved icing sugar on top as a garnish.

Cook's tips:
The flaked almonds in the batter are beautiful as they add a wonderful crunchy texture when biting into the soft ricotta filling.

APPLE AND PLUM CRUMBLE (v)

(Serves 4)

1 lb (450g) cooking apples, cored and sliced	TOPPING:
	2 oz (50g) butter or soya margarine
12 oz (350g) plums, stoned and cut into quarters	2 oz (50g) demerara sugar
juice of 1 orange	2 oz (50g) medium rolled oats
½ teaspoon cinnamon	2 oz (50g) large rolled oats
2 oz (50g) demerara sugar	1 oz (25g) wholewheat flour
	1 oz (25g) ground almonds
	3 dessertspoons water

1. Preheat the oven to 400°F/200°C/Gas Mark 6.

2. Wash and prepare the apples and plums. Place them in an ovenproof dish with the orange juice, cinnamon and sugar. Cover with foil and bake for approximately 20 minutes until the fruit is soft.

3. Place the ingredients for the crumble topping in a bowl (except the water). Rub the fat into the flour, using the same technique as for making pastry. Continue until the mixture is crumbly. Stir in the water. This gives the mixture a more textured appearance on top.

4. Layer the crumble on top of the cooked fruit. Bake for 25 minutes until golden brown on top.

5. Serve hot or cold with whipped cream, custard or Greek yoghurt.

VARIATIONS

APPLE AND PEAR CRUMBLE (v)

1 lb (450g) cooking apples, cored and sliced	1 oz (25g) raisins
13 oz (375g) soft pears, cut in half and cored	juice of 1 orange
	1 oz (25g) demerara sugar

1. Place all the ingredients in an ovenproof dish. Cover with foil and cook for approximately 20 minutes until soft. Finish with topping as with Apple and Plum Crumble.

RHUBARB AND BANANA CRUMBLE

2 lb (675g) rhubarb, peeled and cut into thick pieces	juice of 1 orange
2 large bananas, cut into thick slices	1 oz (25g) demerara sugar

1. Place the chunks of rhubarb plus the orange juice and sugar in a large saucepan. Cook gently until the rhubarb becomes tender, then stir in the slices of banana. Turn into a dish and cover with the topping and finish as with Apple and Plum Crumble.

BLACKCHERRY DELIGHT

(Serves 6–8)

SPONGE BASE:

4 oz (100g) margarine or butter

4 oz (100g) demerera sugar

2 eggs

zest and juice of 1 lemon

4 oz (100g) plain white flour, sieved

1 teaspoon baking powder, sieved

FILLING:

5 fl. oz (150 ml) whipping cream

11 oz (300g) blackcherry yoghurt

2 dessertspoons sugar-free blackcherry jam

7 oz (200g) cream or curd cheese

1 dessertspoon icing sugar

TOPPING AND GLAZE:

8 oz (225g) blackcherries

2 dessertspoons sugar-free blackcherry jam

juice of 1 orange

2 fl. oz (60ml) water

1 level dessertspoon cornflour

1. Preheat the oven to 350°F/180°C/Gas Mark 4.

2. Cut the margarine or butter into cubes and place it with the sugar in a mixing bowl. Using an electric beater (or a wooden spoon), cream the two together until light, creamy and fluffy.

3. Continue beating the mixture whilst adding the eggs, one at a time, beating well between each addition.

4. Using a metal spoon, fold the flour, baking powder, lemon juice and zest into the mixture until well combined.

5. Bake in a 10 inch, lightly greased dish in the middle of the oven for 20 minutes until golden brown. Allow to cool.

6. To prepare the filling, whip the cream until firm. Fold the cream cheese, yoghurt, blackcherry jam and icing sugar into the cream until well combined and lump-free. Spoon the mixture over the cooled sponge and refrigerate.

7. To make the glaze, place the jam, orange juice and water in a small pan. Bring gently up to the boil. Combine a small quantity of water with the cornflour to form a paste. Drizzle into the boiling jam mixture, stirring all the time until thick and glassy. Allow to cool.

8. Remove the dessert from the refrigerator. Completely cover the top with the blackcherries then drizzle the glaze over them. Return to the fridge for at least 1 hour before serving.

Cook's tips:
This dessert can be made using any summer fruit with a complimentary yoghurt and jam, for example strawberries, blackcurrants, raspberries, blueberries.

FRENCH CROISSANT PUDDING

(Serves 4–6)

4 croissants (a day old or par-cooked are best)	2½ oz (60g) castor sugar
a small quantity of butter	3 oz (75g) raisins
½ pint (300ml) single cream	2 teaspoons lemon juice
¾ pint (450ml) milk	½ teaspoon nutmeg
4 eggs, lightly beaten	

1. Preheat the oven to 375°F/180°C/Gas Mark 4.

2. Cut the croissants diagonally into thick slices. Spread one side with butter.

3. In a 10 inch flan dish arrange the croissants, buttered side up, so that they completely fill the dish (overlap the slices if necessary). Sprinkle with raisins.

4. In a bowl whisk the cream, milk, lemon juice, eggs and sugar together. Gently pour the mixture over the slices of croissant, pressing them down so that they are covered by the egg mixture.

5. Sprinkle with nutmeg. Bake in the preheated oven for 45 minutes, or until the pudding has risen and is firm in the middle.

Cook's tips:
This is wonderful served straight from the oven with ice cream.

LIME CHEESECAKE

(Serves 8)

12 oz (350g) digestive biscuits	**FOR THE FILLING:**
4 oz (100g) melted butter	8 oz (225g) castor sugar
nutmeg	3 eggs, separated
thin slices of lime for garnish	8 oz (225g) curd cheese
1 × 8 inch loose-bottomed, spring-sided tin	3 limes (zest of 2, juice of 3)
	½ pint (300ml) whipping cream
	½ oz (12g) agar flakes

1. Place the digestive biscuits in a food processor and blend until they are crumbs. Turn into a bowl and stir in the melted butter with a pinch of nutmeg.

2. Lightly grease the sides and bottom of the tin. Turn the crumbs into the tin and with your fingers press into the base and up the sides so that it is an even thickness. Chill.

3. Using an electric mixer whisk the egg yolks and sugar together until thick, light and creamy. Add the curd cheese to the mixture and continue to whisk until it is a smooth consistency.

4. In a separate bowl whisk the cream until it is firm. Then fold into the egg and cheese mixture.

5. In a clean, dry bowl whisk the egg whites until they stand up in peaks. Fold into the mixture.

6. In a saucepan place the agar flakes, lime zest, lime juice, plus 1 tablespoon of water. Bring to the boil then reduce the heat and simmer for 5 minutes until the liquid is clear. In a steady stream pour the agar mixture into the cheesecake mixture, gently stirring it in all the time until the agar has been completely incorporated.

7. Pour the cheesecake mixture on top of the biscuit base. Chill for at least 4 hours before serving. Decorate with thin slices of lime.

Cook's tips:
Agar flakes, also known as kanten, are a natural vegetable gel derived from seaweed and are a good vegetarian substitute for gelatine. They are readily available from health food shops.

RASPBERRY AND ALMOND SCRUNCH

This recipe was adapted and tested by Jill Moss,
who is a chef at Food For Thought.

(Serves 6–8)

BASE:

| 2 oz (50g) soya margarine |
| 2 oz (50g) brown sugar |
| 3 oz (75g) jumbo oats |
| 3 oz (75g) porridge oats |
| 3 oz (75g) wholemeal flour |

FRUIT:

3 punnets of raspberries

FRUIT GLAZE:

| 2 dessertspoons raspberry sugar-free jam |
| 4 fl oz (120ml) water |
| juice of ½ orange |

TOPPING:

| ½ pint (300ml) whipping cream |
| 1 lb (450g) natural yoghurt |
| 1–2 dessertspoons thick honey |
| juice of ½ orange |
| 2 oz (50g) flaked almonds (toasted under a hot grill for a couple of minutes until golden brown. Cool.) |

1. Preheat the oven to 400°F/200°C/Gas Mark 6.

2. Place the flour and oats in a large bowl. Cut the margarine into chunks and using your fingertips rub the fat into the dry mixture until it resembles breadcrumbs. Stir in the brown sugar.

3. Press into a lightly greased baking tray, so that it becomes the thickness of a biscuit. Bake for 15–20 minutes until lightly golden in colour.

4. Allow to cool, then break into 1 inch pieces (not crumbs) and arrange in a serving dish (a shallow 12 inch dish is ideal). Completely cover the oat base with raspberries, keeping a few back for decoration.

5. For the glaze: place the water, jam and orange juice in a small saucepan. Gently heat, stirring all the time until the jam has melted. When cool, drizzle over the fruit.

6. For the topping: using an electric whisk beat the cream until it stands up in stiff peaks. Stir in the yoghurt, honey and orange juice.

7. Pour the cream mixture over the glazed fruit so that it is completely covered. Decorate the top with toasted almonds and the remaining raspberries. Refrigerate. This dessert is best eaten within 2–3 hours of being made.

Cook's tips:
This is the most popular dessert served at Food For Thought and regular customers will happily eat it every day – the combination of a crisp oat base, soft fruit and a smooth, creamy topping always proves to be a winner.

The fresh fruit filling can be changed according to the time of year, for example slices of fresh peach, thick slices of banana, sliced strawberries or, in fact, any soft fruit, using enough to generously cover the oat base.

The scrunch can also be decorated as flamboyantly as you dare, using melted or grated chocolate, sieved cocoa powder, slices of kiwi fruit, orange segments or the seeds of passion fruit.

RASPBERRY AND HAZELNUT ROULADE

(Serves 4–6)

3 eggs	**FILLING:**
3 oz (75g) castor sugar	8 oz (225g) fresh raspberries
¼ teaspoon vanilla essence	¼ pint (150ml) whipping cream
2 oz (50g) self-raising flour, sieved	icing sugar for dredging
2 oz (50g) ground hazelnuts	

1. Preheat the oven to 400°F/200°C/Gas Mark 6. Carefully grease, line and then grease again a Swiss roll tin or baking tray (34cm × 24cm).

2. Using an electric whisk, beat the eggs, sugar and essence until light and fluffy. Fold in the flour and half the hazelnuts.

3. Carefully spoon the mixture into the tin easing it into the corners. Bake for 7–10 minutes until light brown and firm to the touch.

4. Leave to cool for 5 minutes then turn out onto greaseproof paper. Sprinkle with the remaining hazelnuts. When completely cool spread over the whipped cream, easing it right up to the edges. Sprinkle with raspberries (reserving a few for decoration). Carefully and firmly roll the roulade from the long edge. Trim off a thin slice from each end to neaten it.

5. Decorate with sieved icing sugar and a few raspberries.

SUMMER FRUIT AND MASCARPONE TRIFLE

This recipe was inspired and tested by Louise Hurrell
a regular customer at Food For Thought.

(Serves 4–6)

4 oz (100g) sponge fingers	1¼ lb (575g) mascarpone cheese
2 punnets (250g) raspberries	3 eggs, separated
2–3 oz (50–75g) castor sugar	a dash of liqueur, eg. Cointreau, Grand Marnier (optional)
¼ pint (150ml) orange juice	

1. Lay the sponge fingers in a flan dish or trifle bowl large enough for 4–6 people.

2. Place 1½ punnets of the raspberries, orange juice and 1 oz (25g) of sugar in a saucepan and heat gently until liquified.

3. Pour the fruit (plus a dash of liqueur if required) over the sponge fingers and leave until all the fruit has been absorbed.

4. Place the mascarpone cheese, 1 oz (25g) of sugar and the egg yolks in a bowl and beat together until smooth.

5. In a separate bowl, whisk the egg whites until stiff. Gently fold the egg whites into the cheese mixture until thoroughly combined.

6. Generously spread the mascarpone mixture over the sponge fingers and fruit. Decorate by scattering the remaining raspberries over the top.

7. Refrigerate for approximately 1 hour before serving.

Cook's tips:
Mascarpone cheese has a very luxurious flavour but with 90% fat it is neither cheap nor sparing in calories. However, it is truly worth the indulgence!

THREE LAYER CHOCOLATE MOUSSE

(Serves 6)

17 fl oz (500ml) whipping cream	4½ oz (125g) white chocolate
4 oz (100g) plain chocolate	3 egg yolks
4 oz (100g) milk chocolate	

1. Break the milk chocolate into pieces and place in a bowl over a saucepan with a small amount of water in it to form a bain-marie. Heat gently until the chocolate has melted. Allow to cool.

2. Whisk one third of the cream until it is thick. Stir one of the egg yolks into the chocolate mixture. It will immediately go firm.

3. Using an electric whisk on the slowest setting, whisk the chocolate mixture into the cream until it is smooth. Divide the mixture between 6 ramekin dishes. Refrigerate for 30 minutes. Repeat the whole process using the white chocolate. Very gently spoon on top of the milk chocolate ensuring that there is a crisp line between the two layers. Refrigerate for a further 30 minutes.

4. Repeat the process using the dark chocolate. Again, gently spoon on top of the white chocolate so that there are now three layers. Refrigerate for another 30 minutes before serving.

Cook's tips:
It is essential to refrigerate between each layer of chocolate as this stops the different chocolates from merging into each other and ensures a sharp line between the layers.

This recipe is wonderful but extremely rich and perhaps should only beserved to real chocolate freaks!

TIRAMISU

(Serves 6)

4 eggs, separated	1½ oz (60g) castor sugar
3 oz (75g) bittersweet chocolate, grated	8 oz (225g) mascarpone cheese
	4 oz (100g) cream cheese
9 fl oz (270ml) sherry	2 × 4½ (125g) packets of sponge fingers
9 fl oz (270ml) strong espresso coffee, cooled	

1. Layer half the sponge fingers in the bottom of a deep dish. Soak with a mixture of half the coffee and half the sherry.

2. Whisk the egg yolks and sugar together until light and creamy. Continue to whisk while adding the mascarpone and cream cheese until the mixture is smooth.

3. Whisk the egg whites until they stand up in stiff peaks. Gently fold into the mascarpone mixture. Place half of this mixture on top of the sponge fingers then sprinkle with half of the grated chocolate.

4. Repeat to make one more layer of sponge fingers and mascarpone mixture. Finish with a layer of the remaining grated chocolate.

5. Cover with cling-film and refrigerate for at least one hour before serving.

Cook's tips:
This recipe can be made completely with mascarpone cheese but I prefer to use some light cream cheese to make it less expensive and lower in calories.

WHITE CHOCOLATE AND BAILEYS CHEESECAKE

(Serves 8–10)

PASTRY:

9 oz (250g) white flour

2 oz (50g) castor sugar

pinch of salt

4 oz (100g) unsalted butter

4 tablespoons cold water

an 8 inch loose-bottomed, spring-sided tin

small quantity of white and milk chocolate for garnish

FILLING:

2 oz (50g) castor sugar

2 eggs

12 oz (350g) cream cheese

8 oz (225g) white chocolate

4 dessertspoons Baileys Irish Cream

3 dessertspoons cornflour

1. Preheat oven to 375°F/180°C/Gas Mark 4.

2. Make the pastry by sieving together the flour, sugar and salt. Cut the butter into cubes and add to the flour. Lightly rub the fat into the flour until the mixture resembles breadcrumbs. Add the water and mix lightly to make a soft dough. Cover and leave aside for 15 minutes to allow it to 'rest'.

3. Grease an 8 inch loose-bottomed, spring-sided tin. Roll out the pastry and line the bottom of the tin. Prick it all over with a fork and bake for 10 minutes. The pastry at this stage will not be fully cooked. Reduce heat to 300°F/150°C/Gas Mark 2.

4. With an electric whisk beat the eggs and sugar until light and creamy. Keeping the whisk going add the cream cheese and beat until the texture is smooth.

5. Break the chocolate into pieces and place in a bowl with the Baileys Irish Cream. Place the bowl in a saucepan which has 2 inches of water in it. Heat, stirring the chocolate until it has melted (it will resemble a soft ball).

6. Using an electric mixer beat the chocolate into the cheese and egg mixture until it is a smooth consistency. Add the cornflour to the mixture.

7. Turn the mixture into the pastry case and bake for 30 minutes until the top is lightly golden. Chill for at least 4 hours before serving.

8. Decorate the top of the cheesecake by using a potato peeler to shave off strips of chocolate.

Cook's tips:
This is a delicious but rich dessert so smaller portions are advised!

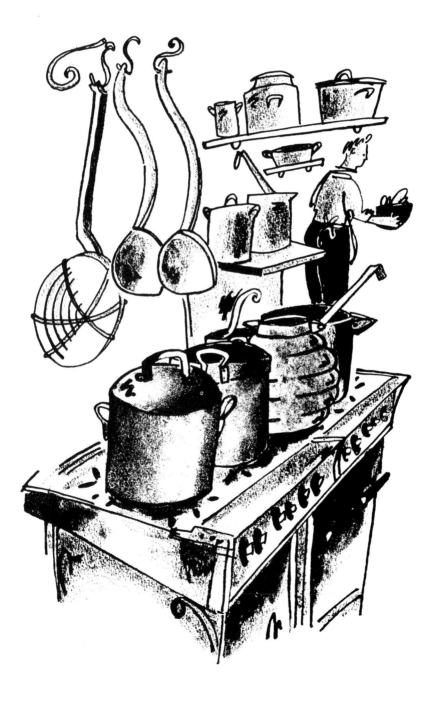

INDEX

INDEX TO RECIPES

INDEX TO VEGAN DISHES

SOUPS:

SALADS, DRESSINGS AND DIPS:

MAIN COURSES:

BREADS, CAKES AND DESSERTS: